Best Friends

Tons of crazy, cool things
to do with your girlfriends

Best Friends

Tons of crazy, cool things to do with your girlfriends

Lisa Albregts & Elizabeth Cape

CHICAGO REVIEW PRESS

Library of Congress Cataloging-in-Publication Data

Albregts, Lisa, 1968-
    Best friends: tons of crazy, cool things to do with your girlfriends / Lisa Albregts
and Elizabeth Cape—1st ed.
        p.   cm.
        Summary: A collection of fun things for girls to do together, grouped by seasons
and including a day of beauty, bicycle road rally, book group, and a sock hop.
        ISBN 1-55652-326-2 (pbk. : alk. paper)
        1. Girls—Recreation—Juvenile literature. 2. Female friendship—Miscellanea—
Juvenile literature. 3. Creative activities and seat work—Juvenile literature. [1. Amuse-
ments. 2. Recreation. 3. Handicraft. 4. Friendship.]   I. Cape, Elizabeth, 1967– II. Title.
GV183.A53   1998   98-25691
796'.083—dc21   CIP
                                                                     AC

Interior design by Mel Kupfer

First edition
Published by Chicago Review Press, Incorporated
814 North Franklin Street
Chicago, Illinois 60610
ISBN 1-55652-326-2

Printed in the United States of America
5 4 3 2 1

For Doug and Sam, who inspire me every day.

L. A.

For all our friends, who have helped us experience
the wonder of friendship. And for Dan,
the craziest, coolest friend I've got.

Ɛ. C.

Contents

🦋 Spring

Summer

Fall

❄ Winter

Introduction

A friend brings you comfort, happiness, and understanding. She is your most trusted ally, your partner in crime, and your biggest fan! She's the one you tell your secrets to, the soul you share your dreams with, and the person who makes you laugh the loudest.

The two of us have been friends for years. We've shared joyful times, sad moments, happy memories, and a whole lot of fun! If there's one thing we've learned, it's that friends are invaluable.

In fact, we could not have written this book without each other. Writing it has been the ultimate friendship project.

Throughout the book's creation we had to be dependable, supportive, and patient. We had fun and we became better friends because of it. Who could ask for anything more?

Well, we can. We ask that you have fun and enjoy this time together. The activities in this book are meant to bring you closer to your friends, and help you welcome new ones. Choose the ideas you like, and go wild with them. After all, friendship is creative and spontaneous. Its rewards are limitless.

We hope that you treasure your friendships as we treasure ours.

Spring

A friend is honest, a friend is kind
A friend can be called on at any time.
Summer, fall, winter, or spring
With each season friendship brings
A thoughtful word, a helping hand
A trusting voice that understands
A loving smile, a silly giggle
Someone who can wag your wiggle!
Spring is fresh and spring is new,
You and your friend have lots to do.
So don't waste a minute
It's time to start.
Plant the seed of friendship,
And let it grow in your heart!

Day of Beauty

Spring has sprung! You may have been hibernating all winter long, but now is the time to gather your friends together and rejuvenate your mind and body. After working hard at school all week, you deserve a day to relax and renew your spirits. You and your friends can pamper each other with soothing activities—from manicures to massages! You can create your very own "day spa," a place to revitalize your skin, hair, and muscles while easing your tired brain.

Before you begin, make yourself warm and comfy by applying sweet-smelling body lotion to your skin and wrapping yourself in a soft robe and slippers. Then let the relaxation begin!

Banana Mask

To take care of your skin, moisturize the natural way. Bananas are rich with vitamin A and potassium and are perfect for a refreshing facial mask. Simply mash a banana in a bowl with a dash of honey and a dash of cream. Mix them thoroughly and smooth the paste all over your face (pull your hair back or wrap it in a towel to keep it out of the way). Leave the mask on for 10 minutes and then rinse with warm water.

Yogurt Hair Conditioner

You can smooth and brighten your hair with this nourishing blend. Beat the yolk of one egg and mix it in a small bowl with one carton of plain yogurt. After shampooing your hair (or shampooing each other's hair like they do at salons), comb the yogurt conditioner through and let it sit for 10 to 15 minutes. Rinse your hair thoroughly with cold water. Ah, what a difference an egg makes!

Manicure and Pedicure

Here are a few steps to a great manicure (trimming and polishing your fingernails). Be sure to ask your parents' permission first—and use clear polish for a fresh and natural look. Take turns giving each other manicures and remember these secrets to great "hand care." First, massage your friend's hands with lotion and wrap warm, moist towels around them to keep her nails soft. Begin by using a nail file (sometimes called an emery board) to give her nails shape, either round or square. You can use a nail clipper if you have a nail that is too long to file down. Once you have finished shaping the nails, you're ready to polish. Paint each nail slowly and carefully and have a cotton swab and some nail polish remover near by in case you make a mistake. Allow her nails to dry for 15 to 20 minutes before you swap places. Run cold water over your nails or blow on them gently to help them dry.

It's fun to give each other pedicures too (trimming and polishing your toenails). Feet are too often forgotten about. Here's your chance to pamper your tootsies and let them know you care. The secret to a perfect pedicure lies in the soaking before you begin. Run warm water in your bathtub, add a bit of mild soap, and soak your feet for 5 to 10 minutes. For extra special pampering, fill a pan or bowl with marbles and rub the bottoms of your feet over the marbles for a soothing massage. Have warm, dry towels available, then massage, trim, and polish just as you did with your hands above. Hint: When you polish your toenails, place a cotton ball between each toe to prevent the polish from smudging.

Finish your day at the spa with a body massage. This is a great way to relax and give your body a special treat. Take turns massaging shoulders, neck, head (scalp massage feels great), arms, and back. The key to a great massage is a strong but gentle touch. Play quiet, soothing music and take time to daydream a bit!

Super Slumber Parties

Isn't it funny that we call overnight parties with our best friends "sleepovers" or "slumber parties," when there is usually very little *sleeping* involved? We hope that the next few activities will keep the girls at your next party laughing and snacking all night long.

Talent Show

They say "there's no business like show business," so put your talents to the test and ham it up. Each girl can take turns performing her particular talent—whether it's singing, magic tricks, dancing, playing an instrument, or doing a cheerleading routine. Or you can work together to perform a group piece for an audience of your family and friends.

Let's say you want to perform a funny skit. Where should you begin? There are so many different ways to come up with skit ideas. The key is to let your creativity go wild. When Lisa was a camper at Camp Minikani, she and her friends would put on skits during campfires. With the help of their coun-selors, they would build blazing campfires and all the campers would perform skits and songs for each other. The girls would work together to write the skit, often using characters from television shows or changing the words to popular songs or doing a dance routine with wacky costumes. The sky is the limit when you're writing together because there are so many ideas and lots of energy. It's important to listen to everyone's contribution and make sure that all ideas are listened to.

Celebrity Match-Up

Gather together your favorite magazines, get out the scissors and start clipping. Ask each girl to cut out five to ten pictures of her favorite celebrities. But here's the trick—cut out only the bodies without the faces. Write the name of the celebrity on the back of the cutout. When you are ready to go, just have each person hold up the celebrity body and all the rest can guess who it is. See how well you know your favorite stars!

What's Your Best Sense?

This game will test four of your five senses: taste, touch, smell, and sound. Gather items from around your house that fall into each sense category (for example, food and drink for taste, small objects and finger foods for touch, spices and soaps for smell, CDs or cassette tapes for sound). One by one, blindfold each friend and ask her to test her senses. Have her taste a cereal flake, and see if she can determine what cereal it is. Hand her a bowl full of fruit and see if she can guess which is which by touch or by smell. Ask her to smell a jar of oregano and guess the spice. Then play very short clips from your favorite CDs or tapes and ask her to guess the band. You'll see that when you are blindfolded, your other senses become sharper. You are forced to pay greater attention to smell, taste, touch, and sound.

Sleepover S'Mores

When you and your buddies get the slumber party munchies, there is nothing better than a plate of ooey, gooey Sleepover S'Mores. And the great thing is, you don't need a campfire to make these little goodies.

You will need
- Graham crackers
- Microwave-safe plate
- Marshmallows
- Milk chocolate candy bar squares

Place some graham crackers on a microwave-safe plate. Top each cracker with a marshmallow and a chocolate square. Microwave for 20 seconds, or until the marshmallow is soft. Place another graham cracker on top and squish slightly.

Variations

PBJ-A-OKs: Add a teaspoon of peanut butter and a teaspoon of strawberry jelly for a terrific change of pace.

Monkey Business: Add a slice of banana for a fruity treat.

Minty Melty: Instead of the chocolate square, add a chocolate-covered peppermint patty. It's delicious when it's gooey.

Coconutty S'Mores: Top your S'more with a sprinkle of coconut for a tropical taste.

Fastest Donut in the West

This is a fun game to play at a slumber party breakfast. Two friends will enjoy it, or you can play with a larger group of guests. If you plan on staying up all night and think you might be too groggy in the morning for a race, try playing it before "bedtime."

You will need
- String
- Regular old donuts with holes in the middle (no donut holes or fancy fillings)
- Long pole or broom handle
- 2 stools
- Masking tape

1. Tie a string to a donut and then tie the string to the pole.
2. Tie another string to another donut and tie this string to the pole. Make sure that both donuts hang the same distance from the ground. Hang the donuts so that there is about 1½ feet between them.
3. Add more strings and donuts if more than two people are playing.
4. Place each end of the pole on a tall stool so that the donuts can swing freely. They should be at about mouth level when you're sitting on the floor. Tape the ends of the pole securely to the stools.
5. Each person should sit cross-legged in front of a donut.
6. Players should count down from five and when they get to zero, start nibbling away.
7. The first person to eat the entire donut, wins!

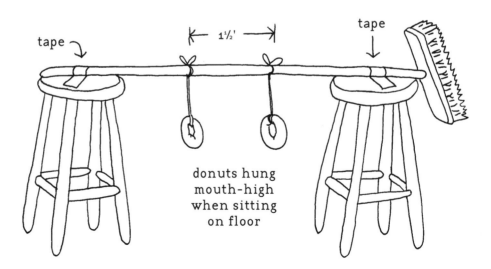

tape

1½'

tape

donuts hung
mouth-high
when sitting
on floor

Capture a Moment in Time

Imagine how much fun it would be to open a time capsule from many years ago! You might find letters, newspaper articles, or photographs that give you insight to a different era. You and your friends can make time stand still (if only for a moment) as you capture your feelings, fashions, and favorites of the day.

You will need
- Pens or markers
- Writing paper
- A sturdy box or plastic container
- Thick tape

Ask each of your friends to write a note about how they feel on this day. What special things are happening in their lives? What do they like to do for fun? Who do they have a crush on? What do they hope to be when they grow up? Then make a list of "favorites" and have everyone answer them—what is your favorite ice cream flavor? book? pizza topping? Then fold up each note and place it in the box.

Add all of the other mementos you would like to include. (See the list below for ideas.) Close the box and seal it securely with tape. Write today's date on the box, as well as the date you've decided to reopen the capsule. You can wait for months or years, but the longer you leave the capsule, the more fun you'll have reopening it. Hide the box in a safe place where you'll forget about it for a while.

Ideas for time capsule goodies
- Photographs
- Newspapers or magazine stories
- An audiotape or videotape featuring you and your friends
- Pictures of movie stars and fashion models from magazines
- Theater or movie ticket stubs
- Predictions for the future

Volunteer Project: Food Drive

Throughout this book you will find volunteer projects that you can organize with your friends. We believe that one of the best ways for friends to spend time together is while working for a greater cause. You will always have time to go shopping or talk about boys or see a movie. But when two or three or ten of you come together to help out others, it is an experience you will never forget.

Food pantries are organizations that provide free food and meals to people who are in need. The pantries receive lots of attention during the holiday season, but they are often short on basic food supplies during other times of the year. You can contact your local food pantry or aid center to find out what kind of foodstuffs they need. (Use the telephone book, or call your community city hall for pantry locations in your area.) Then you and your friends can gather food using one of the following activities.

Food Scavenger Hunt

Make a list of nonperishable food items (foods that do not need refrigeration), such as canned soups, pasta, dry cereal, and canned fruits and vegetables. Split your friends into teams and copy the list so that each team gets one. Do whatever you can to gather all the food items on your list. Stop at your own homes to ask for a contribution, knock on your neighbors' doors, or call friends who might be willing to bring cans or boxes to school the next day. The "winning team" is the one who finds all of the items first, but everyone wins for taking time to help others.

Start a Food Drive at School

After speaking with your teacher or principal, work with your classmates to gather food at your school. Make posters and flyers announcing the day that food will be collected. Word of mouth is key! Get your school excited about the volunteering spirit. Decorate large, clean garbage cans for collecting all the food and ask for help from teachers or parents to transport the food to the pantry.

EVERY LITTLE BIT HELPS

You may feel like your contribution is just a drop in the bucket, but you can make a difference in the lives of others. Recently, we heard a story of a ten-year-old girl in Houston, Texas, who collected loose change – pennies, nickels, dimes, and quarters – from everyone she met for four years. She raised more than $10,000, which she gave away to charities all over her state. She is a shining example of how little acts of kindness can grow and flourish.

I alone cannot change the world, but I can cast a stone across the waters to create many ripples.

— MOTHER TERESA

Trading Treasures

Get together with your best friend and transform an ordinary cardboard box into a beautiful Treasure Box. And then let the real fun begin! Take turns filling the box with meaningful treasures and then leaving it for each other to find. We've all had days when we could use a cheery surprise. Let's say you've got the Box and your friend's got a math test coming up. Wouldn't she love to find a Treasure Box filled with little treats in her locker on test day? The Box then becomes her responsibility, and she will find a time and a place to leave you a special surprise. See how long you can continue exchanging your Treasure Box! Liz's Great Uncle Buddy and Grandma Dottie did it for more than twelve years! Wow!

You will need

- Brightly colored tissue paper (use colors that go together well)
- Newspaper
- 2 sponge brushes
- Gloss Mod Podge (from an art or craft supply store)
- Small cardboard box with a lid (empty candy boxes work well)

1. Rip the tissue paper into small pieces about the size of a half-dollar.

2. Cover your workspace with newspaper. Use the sponge brushes to spread thin coats of Mod Podge onto the outside of the box and its lid.

3. One friend can decorate the box and the other can decorate the lid. Place pieces of tissue paper onto the wet Mod Podge. Gently brush a little more Mod Podge on

top of the tissue paper. Keep adding and overlapping pieces of tissue paper until you have covered every bit of the box and lid. Remember to brush a little more Mod Podge on top of each piece of paper you add. This will help it stick.

4. Let the decorated box and lid air dry for about 2 hours.

5. When your Treasure Box has completely dried, decide who is going to keep it first. At every exchange, write the date inside the lid. Have fun being sneaky by surprising each other throughout the year!

**The only reward of virtue is virtue;
the only way to have a friend
is to be one.**

—Ralph Waldo Emerson

Flower Child Face Painting

In the late 1960s, kids were digging bands like Jefferson Airplane, the Grateful Dead, the Beatles, and the Byrds. The music was psychedelic and their clothes were supermod. Bell-bottoms, crocheted vests, and miniskirts with platform shoes hit the fashion scene. Hippies were flashing peace signs and gigantic smiles. During the Summer of Love in 1967, the young faces of some flower children were filled with painted peace signs, stars and moons, and, of course, flowers. Take turns using each other's faces as canvases and transform yourselves into really groovy girls for a day!

You will need
- Hand lotion
- Small bowls for mixing
- Spoons
- Dry tempera paints in various colors
- Cotton swabs
- Baby shampoo

Squeeze some hand lotion into a small bowl. Add a teaspoon of dry tempera paint and mix. If the shade is too light, add a little more paint. If it is too dark, add a bit more lotion. Mix several different colors. It is important to spread a little face paint on the inside of your forearm to see if your skin is irritated by the paint. Remove it and wait a while to make sure the face paint doesn't irritate your skin. When you're ready to decorate your faces, spread a thin coat of lotion on first. Then dip cotton swabs (or fingers for a different effect) into the mixtures and apply to your partner's face. Take turns painting simple flowers, hearts, swirls, stars, suns, moons, happy faces, and peace signs on each other's faces. Don't stop until you both look too far out for words. Yah, baby! To clean up your faces, use a little water and baby shampoo.

GET JIGGY WITH IT

Every generation invents its own colorful slang words. That was certainly true for young people in the sixties! They came up with words like "hip," "fab," "mod," "far-out," and "groovy" that all meant that something was cool. If you really liked something you "dug" it. Back in those days, you might have heard, "I dig that new Beatles song, 'A Little Help from My Friends'!" Can you think of some of your generation's slang words?

Spring Teepee

So you say you want a place of your own but you're not quite ready to move out of the house and pay rent? We have the perfect solution— build a teepee! It's a perfect little hideaway for two friends to hang out.

You will need

- Utility knife
- 40 feet of rope
- Tall tree
- 4 sturdy sticks
- Several big blankets
- Clothespins

Ask an adult to cut the rope into four 10-foot lengths and then to tightly tie the four lengths of rope 6 feet up the tree's trunk. Pull the loose ends of the rope down and out and tie them securely to the sticks. Push the sticks into the ground. Now cover the form with the blankets. Attaching clothespins here and there will keep the blankets from slipping off.

BOOKS ABOUT SECRET PLACES

These are two fantastic books about friendships and secret places. We encourage you to read *Bridge to Terabithia* by Katherine Paterson and *The Secret Garden* by Frances Hodgson Burnett. Try to get ahold of two copies so that you can enjoy the stories together.

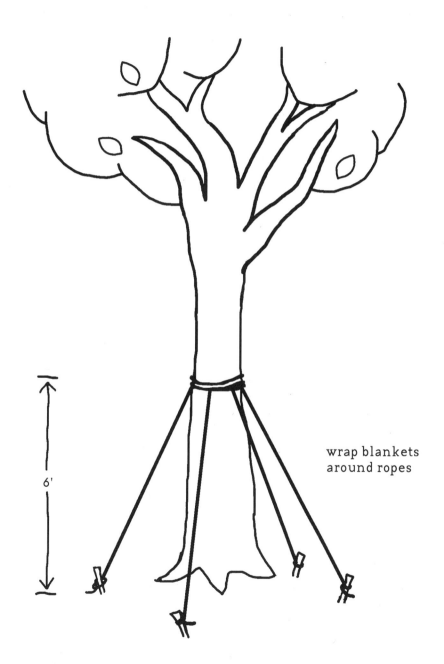

6'

wrap blankets
around ropes

Earth Day Grassy Heads

The first Earth Day was held in 1970 to honor the earth and all of its resources. It was organized by Senator Gaylord Nelson from Wisconsin. He felt it was a great way to remind Americans of how important it is to take care of the earth. People spent the day picking up litter, planting trees, and learning about the dangers of pollution. Decades later, Earth Day is celebrated around the world to remind people that they can help save the planet by producing less garbage, cleaning up the air and water, and using the land wisely. Communities, schools, and families celebrate Earth Day each year on April 22. This project is a perfect way to recycle some things that you might be tempted to toss away. Remember: Earth Day can be *every* day!

You will need
- 1 cup potting soil
- 1 leg of an old, clean pair of nylons
- 1 to 2 tablespoons grass seed
- Permanent markers
- Glue
- Pair of googly eyes (buttons work, too)
- Big jar lid or bowl

Sprinkle ½ cup potting soil in the bottom of the nylon leg. Place a generous tablespoon of grass seed on top of the soil. Pour the remaining ½ cup potting soil on top of the seed. Tie the nylon leg in a knot to make a ball filled with soil and grass seed. Cut the nylons off above the knot. Using permanent markers, draw a face on the Grassy Head. Glue on some googly eyes. Dip the top of the Grassy Head into water so that the seeds get soaked. Place it onto the jar lid or bowl with the top of the head facing up. Find a sunny window to place it in and wait for the "hair" to sprout. Remember to dip the top of the Grassy Head in water every other day so that the seeds stay moist. In about a week, your Grassy Head should have some hair. You might even want to give it a quick haircut. (No blow drying though, please!)

SAVE THE EARTH

Do you know the four R's of ecology? *Reduce* the amount of waste made in the first place by not buying overpackaged materials. *Recycle* items like metals, glass, and paper. *Reuse* things that might be ready for the garbage by using them again in a different way. *Respect* the earth and its resources. Remember – it's only yours to borrow, so save it for tomorrow!

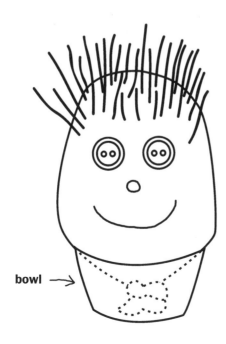

bowl →

E-mail Escapades

E-mail, short for "electronic mail," is a cool new way to correspond with friends through cyberspace! Who would have imagined that kids would be able to send messages from one place to another within seconds using computers? If you're lucky enough to have access to a computer that is "E-mail ready" (check out your public or school library), have fun exchanging communications with your friends. To add to your E-mailing enjoyment, try using some of the "emoticons" and "TLAs" below!

What are emoticons? They are simply emotion icons or symbols. They make a sort of face when viewed sideways. Think of them as shortcuts. When you are trying to communicate how you feel in your E-mail, type these symbols that stand for commonly used sayings and emotions. To create them, search for the punctuation keys on your keyboard. Since your recipient cannot hear the tone of your voice, these little fellas will help them better understand your mood. For example, I might include the following in an E-mail to my coauthor: "I have been working on our book all night. I-O I can't wait to see the finished product! :-)"

Some common emoticons

:-) (happy)	:-() (ouch!)
:-((sad)	:-? (puzzled)
:-‖ (angry)	:-@ (screaming)
:-t (annoyed)	:-O (shocked)
I-) (asleep)	:-V (shouting)
:-D (laughing out loud)	I-O (sleepy)
:'-((crying)	;-) (winking)
:-e (disappointed)	:-} (Hmmmmm)
>:-) (evil grin)	:-C (jaw drops to the floo

TLAs, also known as three-letter acronyms, are another type of shortcut used in E-mail messages. These three-letter codes stand for phrases that you probably use quite often in your letters. You'll notice that there are also some commonly used four-letter codes. Shall we call these FLAs?

Try these TLAs and FLAs

BFN (bye for now)

BRB (be right back)

BSF (but seriously, folks)

BTDT (been there, done that)

GAL (get a life)

HHOJ (ha ha, only joking)

NBD (no big deal)

SYL (see you later)

TIA (thanks in advance)

TTFN (ta ta for now)

TTYL (talk to you later)

TVM (thanks very much)

YMBJ (you must be joking)

A couple of reminders when using E-mail

1. Only write messages to people you know!

2. Be polite.

3. Write your message off-line and then go on-line to send it.

4. Remember, while you're on-line, a phone line is being tied up. Be respectful of others.

5. Make sure that the recipient of your message understands the emoticons and TLAs that you have included!

E-MAIL VERSUS SNAIL MAIL

Which do you prefer — corresponding by way of E-mail or "snail mail"? Snail mail is the nickname given by some to the more traditional way of sending letters through the postal service. We see the pros and cons of both of them. While E-mail is extremely fast and exciting, old-fashioned letter writing seems more romantic and personal. You decide!

Birthday Bags

Spend an afternoon making these bags together. Each of you can then take one of the finished bags home to save until the other's birthday. Before the big day, fill the Birthday Bags with trinkets and treats like stickers, candy, a good book, a cassette tape, a small stuffed animal, or any other little gift that you know your friend will appreciate. Hand-deliver it to the Birthday Girl on her special day!

For two Birthday Bags, you will need
- Colorful fabric, about 24 by 24 inches
- 2 yarn needles
- Yarn
- Scissors
- Glue
- 2 pieces of narrow ribbon, each 30 inches long

1. Cut the piece of fabric in half. Each friend will have a rectangle that is 12 by 24 inches.

2. For each bag, make a 12-inch square by folding the rectangle in half. The back-side of the fabric should face out and the pretty sides of the fabric should be facing each other on the inside. (This may sound crazy, but after you stitch, you will turn the bag inside out and the pretty fabric will be on the outside!) Notice that the bottom of the bag is at the fold. The top of the bag will remain open, and you'll need to sew the sides closed.

3. Thread the yarn needles with yarn and knot the end. Carefully start stitching about 1 inch down from the top of one side of the bag. Stitch through both pieces of the fabric all the way down the side and cut and knot the yarn at the bottom. Do the same to the other side of

the bag, again remembering to begin stitching about 1 inch down from the top. Leave the top of the bag open.

4. Spread a little glue on the top edge of the bag. Fold the edge down toward the outside of the bag. It is important to leave part of the space unglued. This will leave a little "tunnel" for the drawstring ribbon to go through.

5. Do the same to the top edge of the other side of the bag, too. When the glue has dried, turn the bag inside out. Thread the ribbons through the needles and push the ribbon through the "tunnels." Pull the ribbon tight to close the top of the bag and tie it.

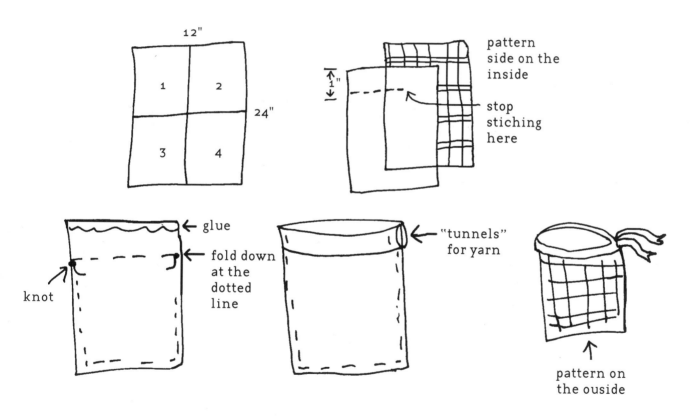

12"

| 1 | 2 |
| 3 | 4 |

24"

1"

pattern side on the inside

stop stiching here

glue

fold down at the dotted line

knot

"tunnels" for yarn

pattern on the ouside

YOU MAY KNOW WHAT YOUR BIRTHSTONE IS, BUT DO YOU KNOW YOUR BIRTH FLOWER?

January – Snowdrop	July – Daisy
February – Carnation	August – Poppy
March – Violet	September – Morning Glory
April – Lily	October – Cosmos
May – Hawthorn	November – Chrysanthemum
June – Rose	December – Holly

Attaching one of these to a Birthday Bag, along with a brief explanation, would be a thoughtful touch!

Chinese Zodiac

According to Chinese astrology, each year is ruled by one of twelve animals. It is believed that everyone has personality traits like the animal that ruled the year they were born. Get together with some friends (perhaps over egg rolls and sweet and sour chicken) and determine which animals reigned during the years you were born! Then do a little dreaming and predict what your future will hold.

1984, 1996—Rat

Rats are imaginative, energetic, and humorous. They make good managers, architects, teachers, and salespeople. Rats prefer the company of Dragons, Oxen, and Monkeys.

1985, 1997—Ox

Oxen are hard working, patient, strong, and easy going. They make successful geologists, dentists, principals, or social workers. Oxen are most compatible with Roosters, Rats, and Snakes.

1986, 1998—Tiger

Tigers are brave, protective, emotional, and daring! Tigers might enjoy becoming reporters, actors, circus performers, or pilots. They enjoy spending time with Horses, Dragons, and Dogs.

1987, 1999—Rabbit

Rabbits are neat, ambitious, and sociable. They are best suited for jobs in nursing, law, banking, or interior design. Rabbits like the company of Goats, Dogs, and Pigs. It must be a barnyard thing.

1988, 2000—Dragon

Dragons are lucky, fun, flashy, and energetic. Dragons make good professional athletes, hair stylists, and television anchors. They feel comfortable with Tigers and Rats.

1989, 2001—Snake

Snakes are quiet, thoughtful, and mysterious. They are happy as counselors, playwrights, photographers, and librarians. Snakes enjoy the company of Roosters, but are best suited for an Ox.

1990, 2002—Horse

Horses are cheerful, showy, vivacious, and dedicated. They make good astronauts, dancers, astrologers, and musicians. Horses make good partnerships with Rams, Tigers, and Dogs.

1991, 2003—Ram

Rams are gentle, artistic, caring, and charming. Rams might make good therapists, authors, artists, or florists. Rams will find true happiness if they marry a Rabbit, Pig, or Horse.

1992, 2004—Monkey

Monkeys are intelligent, independent, and mischievous. They make great directors, chefs, politicians, and doctors. Monkeys are quite compatible with Dragons, Rats, and Tigers!

1993, 2005—Rooster

Roosters are neat, confident, outspoken, and detail-oriented. They are well suited to be engineers, real estate agents, editors, and travel agents. Roosters get along very well with Oxen.

1994, 2006—Dog

Dogs are unselfish, alert, and dependable. Dogs make good philosophers, judges, activists, or secretaries. Dogs will be happiest with Horses, Tigers, and Rabbits.

1995, 2007—Pig

Pigs are cheerful, trusting, sensitive, and good-natured. They will be successful as inventors, entrepreneurs, tour guides, and psychiatrists. Pigs enjoy the company of a Dragon or a Rabbit.

After you've all had a good laugh, make some predictions for the future. Ask these questions: Do your character traits match with those of the animal that ruled your birth year? What do you want to do when you're an adult? Where do you want to live? Will you live with, near to, or far from your friends? What do you dream for your future? (And most importantly, are there any egg rolls left?)

Friendship Masks

People have created masks throughout the ages for ceremony and celebration. You and your friend can create special masks for one another—wild, funky masks that capture the essence of your personalities.

Before you begin to "create," sit across from your friend and study her face. Start with her basic features: hair, skin and eye color, nose, lips, and ears. Think about things around your house or yard that might be used to represent these parts of her. Really stretch your imagination. Instead of using red yarn for auburn hair, think about the shape and length of her hair and find something that "says" her hair as you see it. Perhaps a combination of flowers and leaves could represent her hair, candy kisses for her ears and bright blue antique buttons for her eyes. The artistic materials should represent not only her realistic features, but also her unique personality.

You will need
- Various objects for the decorative features (see suggestions below)
- Rubber cement
- Something for the base (see suggestions below)
- Paint or markers

Ideas for the decorative features
- Tin foil
- Ribbons, pieces of cloth, or feathers
- Dry cereal or fruit
- Flowers, leaves, grass, or sticks
- Old buttons, pins, or beads
- Coins, bottle caps, or candy
- Stamps, stickers, or pictures

Ideas for the base

- Piece of smooth wood
- Plastic top from a container
- Metal can
- Wrapping paper or newspaper over cardboard

Lay out the "feature" pieces and try different angles and arrangements. When you have determined the perfect layout for your mask masterpiece, use rubber cement to glue the pieces onto your base. Be sure to take it slow and allow the mask to dry completely. You can use paint or markers to add color and to fill in features. We use the term "mask," but these masks do not need to look like traditional masks with eyeholes to see through. This mask is an artistic interpretation of your friend, her features and her personality.

Every child is an artist.
The problem is how to remain
an artist once she grows up.

—Pablo Picasso

Personalized Pancakes

Have you ever had a breakfast party? Lots of people have dinner parties, but why not be different and invite friends over for the first meal of the day? These pancakes can be the main course. Be sure to serve a variety of fresh fruit and a couple of juices, too.

You will need

- Large bowl
- Pancake mix
- Milk
- Eggs
- Small bowl
- Spoon
- Chocolate milk powder
- Griddle or frying pan
- Cooking oil
- Metal spatula
- Maple syrup

1. In the large bowl, prepare the pancake batter according to the directions. Be sure to make enough batter to feed the amount of guests you have.

2. Pour about ⅓ of the batter into the small bowl and stir in some chocolate milk powder. Add enough powder so that this batter is a deep, dark brown color.

3. Ask an adult to help you with the frying. When the griddle or frying pan is warm, add 2 tablespoons of cooking oil to coat the pan. Then carefully pour about ¼ cup of plain batter onto the griddle for each pancake. (We have found that it is easier to make only one or two Personalized Pancakes at a time.)

4. Immediately scoop out about ⅛ cup of the chocolate batter. With a steady hand, pour the chocolate batter on top of the plain pancake to create your friend's initials on it. You could also choose to make a funky design or a simple smiley face instead.

5. Let the pancake cook for awhile. When you notice lots of bubbles on it, it is time to use the spatula and flip it over.

6. After cooking for 1 to 2 more minutes, check the bottom of the pancake. It should be golden brown.

7. Flip the pancake onto a plate and serve it, warm and drenched in maple syrup, to your breakfast buddies.

BREAKFAST FOR DINNER

You can have breakfast food for dinner too! Whenever Lisa's dad was traveling on business, she and her mom would make pancakes, french toast or waffles for supper. Sometimes she and her sisters would even wear pajamas to the table. It was a fun way to mix up that boring dinner routine.

Bicycle Road Rally

Bike riding is a fun way to exercise with friends. Long rides around the block, on a picturesque trail, or along a bike path are good ways to take in the sights and get your heart pumping. Another way to enjoy your wheels is to invite your friends over for a Bicycle Road Rally. These silly games and courses will challenge and entertain all of you. If the mood strikes you, decorate your bikes for the events.

Balancing Act

While the bikes stand still, see who can balance on them the longest without letting their feet touch the ground. Use the second hand of a watch to time the action.

Bicycle Couriers

This is a game of speed and coordination.

You will need
- 4 paper bags
- 4 clothespins with springs
- Marker
- Sidewalk chalk

- Stopwatch or timer

The bags represent mailboxes and the clothespins represent mail. Write the numbers 1 through 4 (addresses) on the bags and the clothespins with a marker. Using chalk, draw a giant square, at least 25 by 25 feet on a blacktop surface. Place one bag at each corner of the square. The first Courier must clip the clothespins to her shirt. Get ready to time the Courier. When signaled to go, she must ride to a bag, get off the bike, and "deliver the mail" by dropping the appropriate piece of "mail" in the appropriate "mailbox." For example, clothespin #1 must be delivered to bag #1. When all of the mail has been delivered, the Courier should return to a designated starting spot to stop the clock. See who can deliver the mail the fastest.

Squiggly Wigglies

Use chalk to draw a short course on blacktop full of sharp turns and abrupt curves. Divide two dozen eggs up evenly between riders. Mark little chalk X's very near to the course. Place one rider's share of eggs on the X's. One rider at a time tries to ride on the course line without smashing any eggs, keeping the bike's front tire on the course line at all times! Reset the course by placing a new share of eggs on the chalk X's for each rider. The rider who smashes the fewest eggs is the winner.

The Tortoise

Using chalk, draw a starting line and a finish line. All riders begin on the starting line. At the starting signal, everyone rides as slowly as possible toward the finish line. Feet must not touch the ground and everyone must keep moving. The last rider to reach the finish line wins.

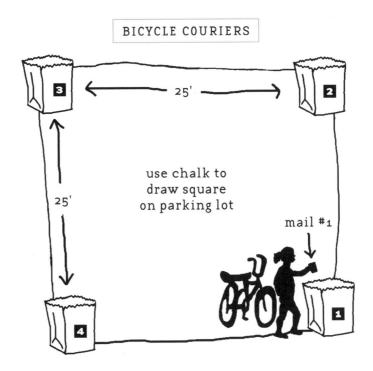

BICYCLE COURIERS

3 — 25' — 2

25'

use chalk to draw square on parking lot

mail #1

1

4

The Hare

This is a game for four players. Split the group of riders into two teams of two and use the starting and finish lines from the Tortoise race. One member of Team A (and one of Team B) stands at a line with a bike. The other member of Team A (and the other Team B member) stands at the other line without bikes. Team members should face each other. When signaled to go, riders jump on their bikes and race to the other line. There, the riders exchange bikes with their teammates. The teammates ride as fast as they can to the other line. The first team to have a member cross this line, wins!

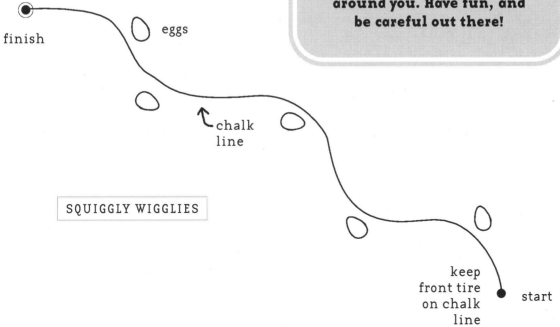

finish

eggs

chalk line

SQUIGGLY WIGGLIES

keep front tire on chalk line

start

Rainy Day Blues

If a rainy day has you trapped indoors, take heart. You and a friend can use this day to set your creative energy free. Listen to the pitter pat of the raindrops on the roof and settle in for a fun day.

Wacky TV Commercials

Look for items around your house that you can write commercials about—toothpaste, cereal, or toys! Or make up your own products with silly names and purposes (like the Mega-Muncher Bagel Maker or Robotic Room Cleaner). Write and act out your commercials for each other or use a video camera to capture the funny commercials on tape!

Name That Tune

Blindfold your friend while you play snippets of music from your favorite CDs or tapes. Play short bits of each song and see how long it takes her to guess correctly. If you have three or four friends involved, you could split into teams and play against each

other, finding out who can name the songs (and the bands) more quickly.

Detective Game

Sit across from your friend and study everything about her appearance—clothing, hair, and jewelry. You'll need a keen eye to be a good detective. She will then leave the room and very sneakily change something about herself. She might take out an earring or roll down her sock. When she comes back, you must guess what it is that she altered.

Volunteer Project: Helping Girl's Best Friend

They say dogs are *man's* best friend, but we know better. Dogs are friends to everyone and we love them because they're cuddly, happy, and loyal. There are many ways to help out the dogs in your neighborhood. You and a friend could volunteer to walk your neighbor's dog for a week or two. You could both volunteer at a nearby animal shelter. Or you could simply whip up a batch of these tasty puppy treats for your favorite brown-eyed, big-pawed friend.

Healthy Puppy Treats

You will need

- Bowl
- 2 eggs
- Fork or whisk
- ⅔ cup whole wheat flour
- ⅔ cup yellow cornmeal
- ½ cup shelled sunflower seeds
- 2 tablespoons corn oil
- ½ cup low-salt beef broth
- ¼ cup milk
- Rolling pin
- Cookie cutters
- Baking sheets

Preheat the oven to 350 degrees. In the bowl, beat one egg with a fork or whisk. Mix in the whole wheat flour, yellow cornmeal, and sunflower seeds (make sure you buy the kind without shells). Add the oil, beef broth, remaining egg, and milk. Mix well and let sit for 15 to 20 minutes. Then use your rolling pin to roll the dough out on a flat surface. Use cookie cutters to cut out fun shapes. Or twist the dough into dog bones by rolling out short pieces of dough and adding round dough pieces to each end. Place the doggie cookies on baking sheets and bake in the oven for 25 to 35 minutes or until golden brown. Always be careful when using the oven and ask an adult to help you.

SILLY PET TRICKS

Another way to have fun with your four-legged friends is to put on your own dog show. Ask all of your friends who have dogs to get together at a park or in a big backyard. Then you can watch each dog perform tricks. But for some dogs the real trick just might be getting them to perform at all! Some puppies are simply best for cuddling.

Sometimes an animal can be your best friend. Here are some of our favorite books about animal friendships.

Where the Red Fern Grows by Wilson Rawls

Charlotte's Web by E. B. White

The Trouble with Tuck by Theodore Taylor

Shiloh by Phyllis Reynolds Naylor

Black Beauty by Anna Sewall

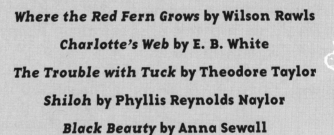

Victory Vegetable Garden

In the 1940s, American soldiers were fighting overseas in World War II. Back home in the states, families were growing their own fruits and vegetables to help the war effort. By producing and eating their own foods, Americans were allowing the regular food supplies to go to the soldiers abroad. Planting a little garden is a lot of work, but it's also a lot of fun. It's the perfect project for a couple of friends.

You will need
- Shovel
- Dry garden fertilizer (from a lawn and garden, hardware, or grocery store)
- Easy-to-grow vegetable seeds (such as carrots, green beans, cucumbers, or tomatoes)
- Ruler

1. Dig up a garden plot. This is a good time to ask for an adult's help. They can help you determine the size of the plot, and help you dig for a while! It's a good idea to keep it small. Loosen the soil to a depth of 6 to 8 inches so that your plants' roots can grow well.

2. As you dig, use a shovel to mix in some dry fertilizer. This will make the soil rich.

3. Carefully read the planting instructions on the seed packets. They will tell you how deep to plant the seeds and how far apart. A ruler might come in handy here.

4. Water the newly planted seeds every day so that the soil surrounding them remains moist. Within a couple of weeks, you should begin to see little sprouts popping through the soil. Keep watering them as they grow into healthy, productive plants. Pull out any strange looking plants you see growing in around your

vegetables because these are probably weeds. (The picture on the seed packet will show you what your plants should look like.)

5. Visit your garden often and watch the changes over time. A couple of months after planting, you'll be able to harvest some vegetables. Enjoy the fruits of your labor by munching them down with some dip!

WHEN TO PLANT?

To learn when to plant your seeds, check the back of the seed packet. It will tell you the best time to plant certain seeds in your area of the country.

Summer

Summer's here and the time is right
For blowin' monster bubbles
And star gazin' at night.
Hangin' with your friend,
Tryin' to beat the heat
Fiesta in your backyard
And a carnival in the street.
Packin' picnic lunches, sippin' lemonade
Summer days are fleetin',
But memories never fade.

Pack a Picnic Lunch

Summer means hot sun, cool shade, and no school! Now that you've escaped those yucky cafeteria lunches, you can surprise a friend with a tasty picnic party. Keep your picnic lunch simple by making foods that you can eat with your fingers, such as sandwiches, sliced fruit or veggies, and sweet treats.

Cool Breeze Lemonade

Makes 2 quarts

You will need
- ½ packet of powdered unsweetened lemonade mix
- ½ packet of powdered unsweetened limeade mix
- 1 cup sugar
- 2 quarts cold water
- Pitcher
- Handful fresh raspberries
- 1 lemon
- 1 lime
- Knife
- Thermos

Mix the powdered drink mixes with the sugar and cold water in a pitcher. Stir it up until mixed well. Wash the raspberries and squish them with the back of a spoon (or your own clean hands), and add to the lemonade mixture. Roll the lemon and lime with the palm of your hand against a clean surface to soften. Then cut each in half and squeeze the juice into the pitcher. Pour into thermos with ice. Yummy!

Turkey Tortilla Roll-Ups

Makes 4 servings

You will need
- 3 tablespoons mayonnaise
- 2 tablespoons tomato salsa

- Small bowl
- 4 large (10-inch) tortillas
- 8 pieces sliced turkey breast
- 4 pieces sliced ham
- 4 slices Swiss or Monterey Jack cheese
- 2 cups washed, shredded green leaf lettuce
- Plastic wrap or tin foil
- Ice cubes in a resealable plastic bag
- Picnic basket
- Dish towel
- Ribbons or flowers

Combine the mayonnaise and salsa in a small bowl. Lay the tortillas out on a clean, flat surface. Spread each one evenly with the salsa mayonnaise. Layer each tortilla with slices of meat and cheese, then top with lettuce. Roll each tortilla up tightly. Wrap the tortillas in plastic wrap or tin foil.

Finally, the most important part of a perfect picnic is the basket! Find a basket of any sort; line the basket with colored tissue paper or a pretty dish towel. Keep the sandwiches cool throughout your picnic by sealing ice cubes in a plastic bag and placing them at the bottom of your basket. String ribbons or freshly picked flowers through the handle and you are ready for a wonderful day.

OTHER PICNIC FAVORITES

Peanut butter and jelly sandwiches with honey or bananas for a change of pace

Bologna and potato chip sandwiches with mustard and lettuce are great!

Egg, tuna, or chicken salad on your favorite bread

Try using a cookie cutter to cut sandwiches into funky shapes — stars, hearts, diamonds, circles, and moons!

DON'T FORGET TO PACK

Blanket to sit on

Paper cups, plates, and napkins

Bug spray

Sunblock

Hats

Kite

Frisbee

Tape player

Monster Bubbles and Best Bubble Hoop

This recipe creates a fantastic bubble solution—just what you and your friends need to make Monster Bubbles some lazy summer day! We've found that better bubbles can be formed if you let the solution "rest" for at least a day. If you have enough patience, let the solution "rest" for up to a week for the strongest and best bubbles possible!

For Monster Bubble solution, you will need
- ⅔ cup Dawn dishwashing liquid
- 1 tablespoon glycerine (from the drugstore)
- 1 gallon water
- Measuring cups and spoons
- Bucket or big bowl
- Shallow tray

Measure the ingredients and mix the bubble solution in a bucket or big bowl. Let the solution "rest" for a day or up to a week. While the solution is resting, you can do two things. 1) Dream of how big and fantastic your Monster Bubbles are going to be, and 2) make a Best Bubble Hoop.

For Best Bubble Hoop, you will need
- Wire coat hanger
- Yarn

Bend the wire coat hanger into a circular shape. You should have a flat hoop with the hook part of the hanger sticking up like a handle. Wrap yarn very tightly around the wire of the hoop. When you dip the hoop into the Monster Bubble solution, more solution will stick to the yarn and this will make better bubbles.

To Make Monster Bubbles

Pour the Monster Bubble solution into a shallow tray. Dunk the Best Bubble Hoop into the solution. Tilt the Hoop around until you have a bubble film extending across it. Gently swing the Hoop through the air, creating a bubble. Carefully twirl the Hoop to seal the bubble off at the end.

BUBBLE SCIENCE

Did you know that a bubble floating freely through the air will always form a sphere? Why? Because of surface tension (the strong attraction of water molecules for each other), a soap bubble always pulls in as tightly as it can, making the smallest surface area possible. Of course, wind or contact with other things will change all of that!

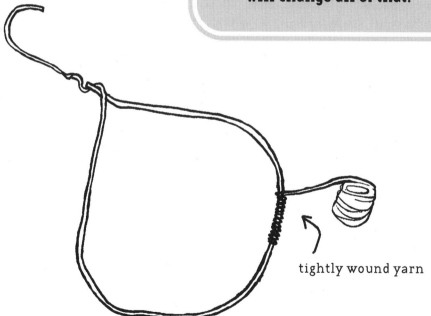

tightly wound yarn

Friendship Bracelets

Friendship bracelets are colorful wristbands that are often exchanged between friends. This bracelet became popular in the 1970s, when it is said that a group of Americans traveling in Guatemala showed some children how to knot the bracelets. The kids caught on quickly and before long, entire villages were knotting bracelets and exporting them to other countries, including the United States.

You and your friends can make a *true* friendship bracelet by working together. Each person chooses a color and the bracelet gets passed around as each friend knots a row in the color she chose. The finished bracelet will be a great example of teamwork.

You will need

- 6 strands of 24-inch-long embroidery thread, of 3 different colors
- Safety pin or masking tape
- Cushion or jeans to pin the bracelet to

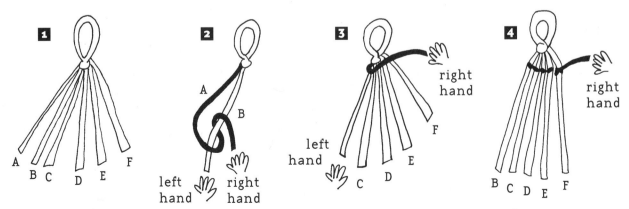

Gather all six strands of thread neatly in your hand and make a loop knot. Pin the loop securely to a cushion or your jeans—or use masking tape and tape the loop to a flat surface—and spread your threads out like a fan.

Assign your threads with letters from left to right, A-B-C-D-E-F. Strings A and D are the same color; B and E are the same; and C and F are the same.

1. Hold A in your right hand and B in your left hand.

2. Wrap A over and under B, pulling the end of A through the loop with your right hand.

3. Holding B taut in your left hand, pull up on A, tightening it into a knot.

4. Repeat, making a second knot with A over B.

5. Drop B and make two knots with A over C. Drop C and make two knots with A over D. Drop D and make two knots with A over E. Drop E and make two knots with A over F. This completes one row.

6. Make the second row by knotting B (now the furthest left thread) over C twice, B over D twice, B over E twice, B over F twice, and B over A twice.

7. Continue in this way until the bracelet is the desired length.

8. Wrap the bracelet around your wrist and tie your loose ends through the loop in a knot.

Remember, be sure to always start with the thread furthest to the left and tie two knots on each thread all the way over to the right.

Loop Knot

1. Fold your threads in half so there is a loop at the top. The ends of the thread should be even.

2. Lay the thread on a flat surface in the shape as shown.

3. Pick up the left half of the bottom loop with your left hand and use your right hand to push the loop under and through the bottom loop.

4. Pull the threads tightly around the loop to form a knot at the bottom of the small loop.

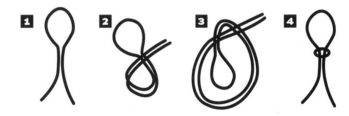

LOOP KNOT

MAKE A WISH

Sometimes these are called Wish Bracelets — if you wear them until the threads break and they fall off, your wish may come true.

Volunteer Project: Carnival for Charity

When we think of carnivals, we think of summer, music, games, costumes, yummy food and drink, and lots of fun. Colorful booths line the street while happy music booms over the crowd. You'll fill the air with festivity when you and your friends bring a carnival to the neighborhood! You can entertain the little kids, amaze the adults, and have a blast doing it. All the while you'll be gathering money from ticket sales to give to your favorite charity.

Your first step is to make posters announcing the big event. Decide the date and time of the carnival, as well as the charity to whom you'll be donating the proceeds. Include all of this information on your colorful posters and hang them all over your neighborhood.

When the carnival day arrives, set up tables outside and decorate them with ribbons and crepe paper. Then fill each table with a different game or challenge. You can charge nickels, dimes, or quarters for each game. Prizes could include stickers, small toys, or candy.

Fortune-Telling

A fortune-teller booth adds an exotic element to any carnival. You can dress up in a colorful, flowing skirt, don your mom's costume jewelry, and sit in a fancy chair. All you need is a crystal ball (a grapefruit wrapped in tinfoil will do), a deck of cards, a flair for the mysterious, and a group of eager carnival goers. Split the deck into two piles: royal cards (Ace, King, Queen, Jack, and Joker) and numeric cards. By choosing cards from each deck and using the chart below, you can peek into each customer's future. (Create your own chart too so you'll have lots of options!)

Ace = Make a wish today and it may come true.

King = You may meet a handsome stranger.

Queen = An important woman in your life will help you this week.

Jack = Adventure is just around the corner.

Joker = You'll soon be involved in a funny or embarrassing moment.

Every card has either a heart, spade, club, or diamond on it (each of these is called a "suit"). Embellish your fortune-telling by studying the suits as well.

Heart = Love
Spade = Mystery
Club = Good Luck
Diamond = Riches

In order to use the numeric cards, create a list of questions that can be answered with a number. For example, "How many children will I have?" or "How many A's will I get on my next report card?" Write these questions down on slips of paper and toss them into a hat. Ask your customer to select a question and then flip over a numeric card. Let's say it reveals a nine of Hearts. You could tell your customer that she'll have nine children (yikes!) and love each of them dearly. Happy fortune-telling!

Send-a-Message

This is a great one for a group of three or four friends to run. All you'll need are slips of paper, pens or pencils, and fast messengers to deliver notes all over the carnival. Carnival goers write messages to friends, family, or crushes and your team of messengers deliver!

Pop the Lucky Balloon

Your carnival goers have one chance to pop the balloon with the lucky red card inside! You'll need to blow up about 15 to 20 dark balloons and place a piece of paper in each. Some will contain lucky red cards. Write a fortune on each piece of paper for the other balloons. Tape the balloons to a wall. Each person has one chance to use a pin to pop open the lucky balloon. If they miss it, they'll still get a fortune. If they find it, they win a prize.

Ideas for more fun carnival games

Ping-Pong Ball Shoot (tossing Ping-Pong balls into wastebaskets)

Sweep the Raisin Race (sweep the raisin across the line first)

Paper Airplane Shoot (fly paper airplanes toward targets for points)

Ping-Pong Ball Maze (see who can blow the ball through the maze the fastest)

Staring Contests (see who can stare the longest without blinking)

Ducky Float (win a prize if you can turn over the rubber ducky with the red dot on the bottom)

Beat the Trivia Genius (wear a turban on your head and use the questions from a question game to stump the crowd)

Other ideas to add atmosphere
- Clowns
- Jugglers (if you're not a great juggler, use handkerchiefs instead of balls)
- A limbo contest
- A food and lemonade stand
- Music, music, and more music—and a place to dance

Beat the Heat

Your hair feels like it's melting. Your parched lips long for a cool drink of water. Your friends are crabby. You need to beat the midsummer heat now! If you've got a long hose and a place to run, you can beat that heat right back to January. (The following three activities are definitely meant for the outdoors!)

Shaving Cream Battle

Don your swimsuits and grab a can of shaving cream. Each of you can take turns "decorating" each other with the foamy white stuff—new hairdos or necklaces will do the trick. Then grab the hose, spray your friends with that cool, clean water and start all over again.

Monkey in the Middle

You'll need at least three people for this game. Fill a few balloons with water and tie them tight. Two girls stand opposite of one another with the third in the middle. As the two girls toss the balloon over the "monkey's" head, the monkey should try to steal the balloon away. Caution: This stealing action may lead to a popped balloon and a very wet, but refreshed friend.

Race of the Hoses

You'll need *two* hoses for this spraying game. The object is to use a hose to push a beach ball across an end line. First set up two end lines parallel to each other and about 10 to 20 feet apart (use jump ropes or string as markers). Each of you should take your places on opposite end lines, facing each other with your hoses ready. Place the ball in the middle of the court and start spraying! The winner is the one who can spray the ball over the opposite end line first! Let the spraying and soaking begin!

Indoor Igloo

Beat the heat with an indoor igloo. Pardon the pun, but this big bubble is really cool!

You will need
- 1 10-by-10-feet or larger plastic drop cloth (from a hardware store)
- Permanent markers
- 1 box window fan
- Roll of duct tape
- A large area with a smooth surfaced floor

1. Spread out the plastic drop cloth on a smooth surfaced floor. You can decorate the plastic with permanent markers for a festive effect.

2. Push the outer edges of the drop cloth in about 2 feet on all sides. The scrunched-in sides will give the bubble room to expand.

3. Stand the fan near one of the drop cloth's edges. Tape the plastic over the outside of the box fan. You do not need to tape the plastic on the bottom side of the fan.

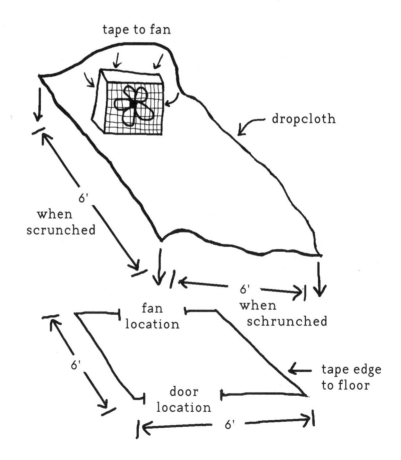

tape to fan

dropcloth

6'
when scrunched

fan location

6'
when schrunched

6'

door location

tape edge to floor

6'

4. Tape the outer edges of the drop cloth to the floor, leaving about 3 feet of it untaped so that you can have a door. Each taped edge will be about 6 feet from its opposite edge.

5. Plug in the fan and turn it on low.

6. Your Igloo should inflate. If there are any holes near the floor (except for the door, of course) tape them so that it is as airtight as possible.

7. When the Igloo is fully inflated, crawl inside. Remember not to turn the fan off when someone is in the Igloo. Also, be sure that when you deflate it no one is inside!

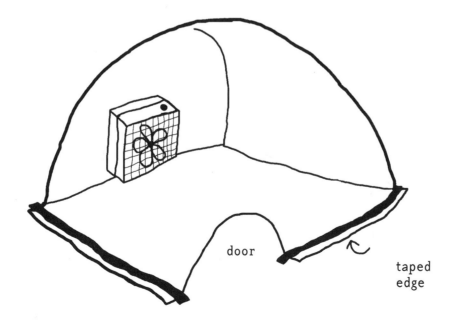

door

taped edge

Sidewalk Acrostics

How about creating a little poetry to dress up a dreary sidewalk? These Sidewalk Acrostics can be a wonderful ode to a friend. An acrostic is a poem in which the first letters of the lines will form a word when you look at them. In this case, that word will be your buddy's name!

You will need
- Sidewalk chalk
- Sidewalk or driveway

Write the letters of your friend's first name on the sidewalk or driveway like we did in our example. Use different colors for each letter. Write them in a big, fancy way! For each letter think of an adjective beginning with that same letter that describes your friend. Here are some acrostics we wrote for each other:

Elegant
Lovely
Interesting
Zany
Amazing
Bubbly
Extra special
Thoughtful
Happy

Loving
Intelligent
Sensitive
Amusing

A Day at the Beach

A day at the beach with friends means cool water, sizzling sand, the smell of sunscreen, and the sound of waves lapping gently on the shore. During your next outing, spend some time gathering tiny treasures to make these enchanting Beach Mementos. They're like snow globes without the flakes! Whenever you're longing for a day seaside, give them a little shake. Reminisce about the fun you had that day with the surf, sand, seashells, and good friends.

Beach Mementos

For each Beach Memento, you will need
- Newspaper
- Spray paint—gold or silver looks great
- Baby food jar with lid
- Tiny treasures from the beach, such as seashells, pebbles, and sea glass
- Small beads and sequins (optional)
- Glitter
- Water
- Clear, 100% silicone sealant
- Glue (optional)
- Paint pen (optional)

Spread newspaper outdoors and spray paint the top of the baby food jar lid. Give the lid about an hour to dry. Then, fill the jar one fourth full with your beach treasures. Add beads and sequins to the water, too, if you like. Sprinkle a little glitter on top. Add water to the very top of the jar. Carefully squirt a small amount of silicone around the rim of the jar. Quickly push the lid onto the jar. Keep it in this upright position overnight until the silicone seals and sets. You may want to use this time to glue beads, shells, or sequins to the lid for decoration. You could even use a paint pen to decorate the jar! The next day, turn your finished Beach Memento over, give it a gentle shake and enjoy the swirling spectacle inside.

ABC Beach Hunt

This is a fun and uncomplicated game that can be played while lounging on a beach towel, lazing under the cool shade of an umbrella, or splashing in the surf. One player starts by scanning the area for something that begins with *A*, for instance, albatross. The next player looks for something that begins with *B*, such as bellybutton! Continue the game, taking turns and moving through the alphabet, until you reach *Z* or until a letter stumps all of the players. If everyone is stumped, you may agree to simply skip that letter and move on with the game. Happy hunting!

Victorian Tea Party

A tea party is a delightful way to spend a summer afternoon. Depending on the weather, your party can be held outdoors, perhaps near a pretty little garden, or indoors. You may either have "tea for two" with your best friend, or invite several acquaintances over for a jolly good time. Be sure to let all of your guests know that "formal" attire is desired. In other words, dig up some lovely dress-up clothes. As you sip and chat, and nibble and visit, pick out royal names for each other such as a Lady Elizabeth or Countess Lisa.

You will need

- Tablecloth
- Napkins
- Fancy teacups and small plates
- Fresh flowers and a small vase (optional)
- Paper doilies
- Herbal tea bags, such as camomile or mint
- Kettle or pot for boiling water
- Teapot
- Sugar
- Milk
- Cookies or Cinnamon Toasties (recipe below)

Set a pretty table with a tablecloth, napkins, and the fanciest teacups and small plates your family will allow you to use. Flowers in a small vase are a nice touch, as are napkins placed to the sides of the small plates. Frilly paper doilies make the table even more elegant. To brew the tea, have an adult help you boil some water in the kettle. He or she should then pour the water into the teapot. Add the tea bags and allow the tea to steep for several minutes. It's a good idea to let the tea cool for several more minutes so that it is easier to carry the teapot to the table. Carefully serve the tea, and encourage your guests to add sugar or milk as needed. Serve some cookies or yummy Cinnamon Toasties.

Cinnamon Toasties

You will need
- White bread
- Toaster
- Knife
- Butter
- Cinnamon
- Sugar
- Cookie cutters

Toast two slices of bread. When they pop up, remove them from the toaster. (NEVER stick ANYTHING, especially silverware, into an electrical appliance like a toaster!) While they are still warm, spread the slices with butter. Sprinkle them with cinnamon and sugar. Use cookie cutters to cut out dainty shapes. Make enough Cinnamon Toasties so that everyone may have three. Serve with tea.

HIGH TEA

Queen Victoria ruled England from 1837-1901. This is known as the Victorian era. She was crowned when she was only eighteen and became the longest reigning queen in England's history! During the Victorian period, afternoon tea might have consisted of tea with cake or biscuits served on the finest china. Victorian ladies followed complicated social rules and were quite concerned with etiquette. At your tea, be sure to employ your very best manners, but have fun. Enjoying tea every afternoon is a timeless British tradition that is still actively enjoyed.

Fourth of July Follies

Isn't it great that there is one day set aside to honor America? The Fourth of July reminds us that the USA is a very special and wonderful country! On July 4, 1776, our founding fathers signed the Declaration of Independence. This date came to represent the birthday of our nation. On this glorious day, we appreciate our many freedoms and let our pride in America show through.

What friends can do to celebrate

- Fly a red, white, and blue kite
- Paint your fingernails to look like Old Glory
- Decorate your bikes with sticker stars and crepe paper stripes
- Pack a picnic lunch with red, white, and blue foods
- Take a walk and count the American flags you see waving
- Braid red, white, and blue ribbons through each other's hair
- Cheer on a Fourth of July parade
- Paint stars on each other's faces
- Tie-dye something red, white, and blue
- Stretch out on a blanket and watch fireworks light up the sky
- Or our favorite . . . make Patriotic Parfaits and Watermelon Stars

Patriotic Parfaits

Makes 2 servings

You will need
- Box of instant vanilla pudding
- Milk
- Tall, clear glasses
- Chopped strawberries or raspberries
- Whipped topping
- Blueberries

Make the pudding according to the directions on the package. Place some pudding in the bottom of each glass. Add layers of strawberries or raspberries, whipped topping, blueberries, and more pudding until you reach the top of the glass. Put one last layer of whipped topping on the very top.

Garnish each Patriotic Parfait with a Watermelon Star.

Watermelon Stars

You will need
- Slice of watermelon (Ask an adult to cut ½-inch-thick circular piece from the melon.)
- Small star cookie cutter
- Plate

Place the slice of watermelon on the plate. Use the cookie cutter to punch out small stars. Use the Watermelon Stars to garnish parfaits, or cut out a whole bunch and eat them as a snack. We dare you to save the seeds for a seed spitting contest later that day!

Tie-Dyed T-shirts

For centuries, people around the world have made their own dyes for coloring fabric and yarn. In fact, people have been dyeing materials for thousands of years in Egypt, Persia, China, and India. Traditionally, insects, plants, shellfish, and minerals have been used to create natural dyes. In 1856, the first synthetic dye was made from coal tar. Since then, such a variety of colors have been created that natural dyes are very seldom used anymore. We've found that beautiful shades of color can be made from synthetic dyes as well. You and a friend can try three different styles of tie-dye: Nigerian, Senegal, and twisted.

For two tie-dyed T-shirts, you will need
- Various colors of bottled synthetic liquid dye (from a craft or grocery store)
- Measuring cup
- Large container of salt
- Several buckets, 1 for each color
- 2 (100% cotton) T-shirts, pre-washed
- Lots of rubber bands
- 2 pairs of rubber gloves
- 2 clothes hangers

Prepare the dye according to the directions on the bottle. Add salt as stated in the directions, as this will help in the dyeing process. Mix one color of dye in each bucket. Thoroughly soak the T-shirts in clean water. You have several choices of tie-dye patterns.

Nigerian Style

Grab and scrunch sections of the shirt and wrap several rubber bands around these bunches of fabric. Repeat this process all over the shirt.

Senegal Style

Lay the T-shirt flat. Starting at the bottom, fold the shirt like a fan—back and forth, horizontally. Wrap rubber bands around the folded shirt in several places.

Twisted Style

Twist the entire T-shirt, including the sleeves. When it is tightly twisted, wrap rubber bands around the shirt in several places.

Pull on your rubber gloves. Now it's time to dip the shirts, or parts of them, into the dye. You may choose to make different parts of your shirt different colors by dipping one section in blue and another in red, for example. The fun thing about tie-dyeing is that you're never quite sure what kind of design you'll end up with. Experiment and have fun!

When you're done dipping, leave the rubber bands on the T-shirt and let it "rest" for about an hour. This will allow the design to set. Then take off the rubber bands, rinse in clean water, and hang the shirts on clothes hangers to dry.

Remember: Always wash these tie-dyed T-shirts separately because the dye might "bleed" onto other clothes!

NIGERIAN

SENEGALESE

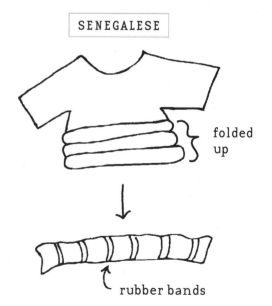

folded up

rubber bands

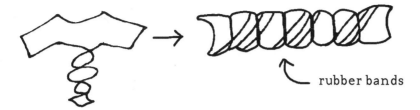

rubber bands

GO NATURAL

For natural dyes mix these ingredients with 1 quart of boiling water. Allow it to steep, then strain.

2 cups crushed, frozen blueberries – BLUE

2 cups canned beets including juice – RED

1 tablespoon turmeric – BRIGHT YELLOW

6 black tea bags – BROWN

1 box frozen spinach – GREEN

3 cups grape juice – PURPLE

A Mexican Fiesta

Want to throw a party that's *muy buena*? Have a Mexican Fiesta! Make some quesadillas, serve tortilla chips in a sombrero with a side of salsa, find some Mexican music at the library, and invite some *amigas* over to party around the piñata!

Quesadillas

Makes 10 servings

You will need
- 16 to 20 flour tortillas
- Baking sheet
- 2 cups grated Monterey Jack cheese
- 2 cups grated Cheddar cheese
- Spoon
- 1 jar of chunky salsa (mild, medium, or hot . . . you pick!)
- Oven mitts
- Knife

Preheat the oven to 350 degrees. Be sure to ask an adult for permission before using the oven. Lay half of the tortillas on a baking sheet in a single layer. Cover each tortilla with a little of each of the cheeses. Put about three spoonfuls of salsa on top of the cheese. Place a dry tortilla on top of each cheesy tortilla. Use oven mitts to put the pan into the oven. Bake for 10 to 15 minutes, or until the cheese is melted. Let the quesadillas cool a bit before cutting them into fourths. Serve with something cold and delicious to drink.

Piñata

A piñata is a decorated container filled with little toys and candy. In Mexico, children enjoy taking a swing at piñatas at parties before Easter and Christmas. Piñatas are hung from trees or the ceiling. Children in blindfolds take turns trying to break the piñata open with a stick! When the piñata breaks, everyone scrambles to collect the treats that were inside. You can make your very own colorful piñata for your fiesta!

This activity will take about two days—one day to make the papier-mâché shell and another to decorate it.

You will need

- Old newspapers
- Big balloon
- Bag of wheat-based wallpaper paste (from a hardware store)
- Bucket
- Empty can or jar (to use as a stand while the papier-mâché shell is drying)
- Wrapped candy
- Duct tape
- Heavy string
- Scissors
- Brightly colored tissue paper
- Glue
- Streamers

To make the shell of the piñata

1. Lay down a few sheets of newspaper to protect the floor.
2. Tear some of the other newspaper into long, thin strips about 2 inches wide.
3. Blow up the big balloon and tie it.
4. Mix the wallpaper paste in the bucket according to the directions on the bag.
5. While one friend holds the balloon, the other will dip the strips, one at a time, into the paste. Carefully shake off any extra paste.
6. Place the strips onto the balloon and smooth. Cover every inch of the balloon, but leave the spot where you tied it uncovered. The uncovered spot should be about 1-inch square.
7. Place the balloon on the can or jar stand and let dry for about 24 hours. When it's dry, there should be no sticky spots!

To decorate the piñata

1. Pop the balloon inside the piñata shell.
2. Fill the shell with wrapped candy and other small goodies.
3. Cover the hole securely with duct tape.
4. Using many pieces of duct tape, securely attach a length of heavy string to the opposite end of the shell.
5. Cut the tissue paper into large squares that are about 6 by 6 inches.

6. Crumple the squares so that they look like flowers.

7. Glue the flowers onto the piñata shell. Cover every inch with tissue paper and flowers so that it looks colorful and festive!

8. Hang some streamers from the bottom of the piñata.

9. Using the attached string, tie the finished piñata to the branch of a tree.

Remember: If a tree is not available, the piñata can be tied to the end of a long pole. Someone will have to hold the pole when it is time to swing at the piñata. Another way to hang the piñata is to string up a clothesline and hang it off of that.

PIÑATA MASTERPIECES

If you'd like to learn more about piñatas, check out the book *The Piñata Maker* by George Ancona. Written in both English and Spanish, it is filled with beautiful photographs that show how El Piñatero makes these creations.

Sol de Mexico

Thousands of years ago, American Indians known as Mayans had a thriving civilization in Central America and southern Mexico. Mayans worshiped many gods and goddesses, one of which was called Kinich Ahau—the Sun God. In more modern times, Mexican artisans began creating brilliant metal tooling crafts like the Sol de Mexico. This activity was influenced by the beautiful sun that has been so inspirational and important to cultures throughout history.

For each Sol de Mexico, you will need
- Pencil
- Unlined paper
- Any size piece of 36-gauge metal: aluminum, copper, or brass (From an art supply store. Or, use very thick aluminum foil or a pie tin.)
- Small stack of newspapers
- Ballpoint pen
- Popsicle stick
- Assortment of permanent markers (We like the HOT colors best!)
- Scissors

1. Draw a simple sun shape on the unlined paper with a pencil.

2. Place the paper on top of the metal piece. Place this on top of a small stack of newspapers.

3. With the ballpoint pen, trace over the drawing of the sun on the paper and press into the piece of metal.

4. Now you'll be creating a design on the inside of the sun's shape. Flip the metal piece over and begin working on the back side. Again, place the metal piece onto the newspaper. Use a popsicle stick to push certain areas of the design out. Push, drag, and smooth the metal any way you like. You'll see that this will cause specific areas of your sun to appear raised on the front. Be careful to stay in the lines!

5. Now you may add texture and designs to your piece. Working from the back side again, use a ballpoint pen to add texture or to push designs into the metal.

6. Using permanent markers (and remember, the hot colors look awesome!), color the front side of your sun.

7. Use the scissors to cut the sun out.

You can glue your Sol de Mexico onto the popsicle stick, or punch a hole in the top for a string to hang, or add a chain and make a necklace. You can make other shapes and give them away as tree ornaments or even make tiny ones for earrings. Make several pieces and create a mobile, or change the shape of your metal tooling (we suggest a narrow rectangle) to make a bracelet.

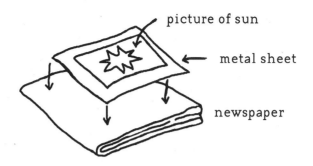

picture of sun

metal sheet

newspaper

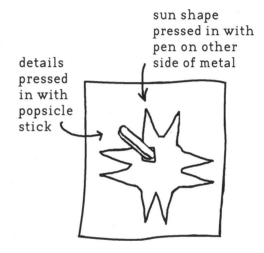

sun shape pressed in with pen on other side of metal

details pressed in with popsicle stick

cut out when finished

LEARN A LITTLE SPANISH

Can you speak Spanish? If not, try using some of these words and phrases at the party!

muy buena (mwee BWAY nah) = very good

sombrero (som BRER oh) = hat

amigas (ah ME gas) = girlfriends

hola (OH la) = hello

¿Que tal? (kay TAHL) = How are you?

muy bien, gracias (mwee be EN, GRAH see us) = very well, thanks

me llamo . . . (may YAH moh) = my name is . . .

¡Hasta pronto! (AH stah PRON toh) = See you later!

adios (ah de OHS) = goodbye

Getting Back to Nature

Overnight camping is so much fun, but you can also have an excellent time on a day camping trip! You don't have to go far to get away and enjoy the great outdoors. Find an interesting spot in your own backyard or at a nearby park. Pitch your tent, go on a nature hike, have a snack, breathe in the fresh air, and enjoy everything our earth has to offer. Don't forget the bug spray and sun block!

Terrific Tent

So, you say you don't have a tent? No problem! Follow these simple directions and you'll have a tent that you can use for day camping in no time at all.

You will need
- 1 piece of rope, 18 feet long
- Big blanket, sheet, or tarp
- Several clothespins with springs
- Several large rocks or bricks

Find two trees that are about 10 feet apart from each other. Tie the rope from one tree to another. Tie it tightly and make sure the rope hangs 4 to 5 feet above the ground.

Toss your big blanket over the rope and secure it in several places with the clothespins. Stretch the blanket out along the ground in both directions as far as they can go. Place the large rocks or bricks (or anything else heavy that you can get your hands on . . . and little brothers don't count) along the edges of the blanket to hold it in this stretched-out position and you've got yourselves one terrific tent!

Natural Scavenger Hunt

After you've settled into your tent, why not go on a scavenger hunt? Make a list of things to find in the area around you. All you need is a piece of paper and a pen.

Our last scavenger hunt list looked like this: To find: an acorn, a stick shorter than your foot, a gray rock, an oval leaf, a pine cone, a leaf with five points, a pine needle, a blade of grass longer than your foot, a flower, a piece of tree bark, and a piece of litter (sad, but true. Do a good deed: Carefully pick up the litter that you find and toss it in a trash can.)

Make sure that each of you has a copy of the list and go! See who can find all of the items and return to the tent first.

Mix-It-Up Trail Mix

This is a great day camping recipe that doesn't require a campfire. Simply choose several ingredients from the lists below, put a scoop or two into a big, resealable bag, and let the ingredients mix up as you carry the bag of goodies to your campsite. Easy and delicious! We wouldn't think of going on a camping trip without some.

TRAIL MIX INGREDIENTS

Nuts and Seeds	Dried Fruits	Treats
walnuts	apricots	chocolate chips
peanuts	bananas	M&Ms
Brazil nuts	apples	Skittles
almonds	blueberries	coconut flakes
hazelnuts	cranberries	chocolate stars
pecans	cherries	malted milk balls
macadamia nuts	pineapple	butterscotch chips
pumpkin seeds	raisins	Frosted Wheat
sunflower seeds	dates	peanut butter chips

For a tropical treat try mixing:	
macadamia nuts	dried papaya
almonds	dried bananas
coconut flakes	chocolate stars

For a mix that tastes a lot like a gourmet caramel apple try:	
peanuts	pecans
dried apples	butterscotch chips
chocolate chips	

Star Gazing

Oh starry, starry night! When there are more stars in the sky than imaginable, grab a blanket and head outdoors. You'll also need a small flashlight and a star map, star finder, or book about constellations. You can pick these up at nature and camping stores, toy stores and bookstores, or your library. You might want to use a pair of binoculars to aid in your star gazing, but they are not necessary. Once you've gathered your supplies, find a quiet spot far from distractions like porch lights and street lamps. Give your eyes some time to adjust to the darkness, and then relax and gaze at a handful of the more than 200 billion (that's 200,000,000,000!) stars in our Milky Way galaxy.

Gazing at Constellations

Thousands of years ago, astronomers grouped stars together to form pictures called constellations. Start your evening of star gazing by finding the Big Dipper constellation. It is easy to find because it looks like a giant soup ladle! The Big Dipper is part of a larger constellation known as Ursa Major, or Great Bear. You'll see that the tail and hips of the Great Bear are actually the Big Dipper. If you follow the two stars at the end of the bowl of the Big Dipper, you'll come to Polaris, or the North Star. Polaris always shines to the north, so throughout history people have used this star to guide them—explorers, hunters, even runaway slaves! Polaris is the last star in the handle of the Little Dipper, also known as Ursa Minor or Little Bear.

Cassiopeia is a constellation that looks like a *W*. In summer, it is found close to the horizon. To find it, follow the two stars at the end of the bowl of the Big Dipper again to Polaris, and then on to the tip of Cassiopeia. Cassiopeia was a boastful queen who was punished by being hurled into the sky. The *W* shape you see is the queen seated on her throne (use your imagination here).

Gazing at Easy-to-Spot Stars

Use the star map, star finder, or constellation book to help you identify other stars and their locations in the sky. In the summer months, you should be able to see some of our sky's largest, brightest stars like Arcturus, Spica, Regulus, and Antares. The three stars Vega, Deneb, and Altair form the summer triangle. Find these bright stars on your star map and then locate them in the giant triangle in the night sky.

When you grow tired of searching, kick back and spend some time simply gazing. Create some of your own constellations with the star patterns you see in the summer sky. Spin some tales to go along with your constellations. Then just let your minds wander and imagine the immensity of space!

FAR-OUT FACTS

The sun is our closest star!

If you traveled 1,000 miles an hour, it would take you 3 million years to reach the nearest star excluding the sun!

Our sun is only a medium-sized star!

Our galaxy, the Milky Way, is one of about 50 billion galaxies in the universe!

Each galaxy has billions of stars held together by gravity!

It would take you more than 3,000 years to count the stars in our galaxy!

Celestial Crystals

These sparkling beauties are so easy to create. You will probably want to make a whole glittering batch of them. This recipe is for one Celestial Crystal. To make more, just multiply the amount of each ingredient by the number of crystals you want to make.

For each Celestial Crystal, you will need

- Metallic pipe cleaner (You can use regular ones, but gold and silver look so much cooler!)
- String
- Pencil
- Quart-size jar
- ¾ cup borax (from the grocery store near the laundry detergents)
- 3 cups hot water
- Newspapers

1. Bend the pipe cleaner into a celestial shape: a star, sun, or crescent moon.

2. Tie one end of a piece of string to a pipe cleaner shape. Tie the other end of the string to a pencil.

3. Hang the shape in the jar with the pencil lying across the top. Wind the string around the pencil to adjust the string so that the shape hangs at least 1 inch from the bottom of the jar.

4. Mix 3 cups hot water with ¾ cup Borax. Pour this solution into the jar so that it covers the shape completely.

5. In about an hour, you'll see crystals beginning to form! Wait at least 24 hours and then remove the crystallized shape from the solution. Hang it over a stack of newspapers to dry.

6. A Celestial Crystal looks beautiful when hung in a sunny window. Try attaching fishing line to yours so that it appears as if it's floating in the sky!

Are You Bored Today?

Sometimes there are days when nothing feels interesting. The phrase "We are so bored!" is ringing through your house. You and your friend can't think of anything to do. That's when the ultimate checklist comes into play. If you can go through this checklist and still not find something to make you happy, there's only one thing left to do—write your own checklist.

Cool things to do

- Sing a duet and record it
- Lay on the grass and look for shapes in the clouds
- Pick wildflowers
- Play a board game
- Have a rummage sale
- Take a walk through your neighborhood and look for things you've never noticed before
- Go bird watching
- Request a song on a radio station
- Go running
- Taste a food you've never tasted
- Plan a sleepover party
- Build a fort in the basement
- Write a story together
- Rearrange the furniture in your bedroom
- Visit the library
- Bake cookies
- Give your pet a bath
- Tell each other scary stories by candle-light
- Roll on something outside: bikes, rollerblades, or skateboards!
- Dress up in crazy costumes
- Plant flowers in a pot
- Make up a secret language
- Put together a new scrapbook
- Play Chinese jump rope
- Blast the music and dance
- Run through the sprinkler
- Visit famous works of art on a cyber tour of the Louvre Museum in Paris: http://mistral.culture.fr/louvre

Kick the Can Ice Cream

This is the ultimate friendship treat. You mix it together, kick it together, and eat it together!

You will need
- Small coffee can with lid
- Large coffee can with lid
- ⅓ cup sugar
- ¾ cup very cold milk
- 1 cup very cold whipping cream
- 1 teaspoon vanilla extract
- Duct tape
- Ice
- 1 cup rock salt
- ½ cup water

Wash out the coffee cans carefully. Place both cans in the freezer while you're measuring your ingredients. The coffee cans need to be very cold. When ready, take turns putting the sugar, milk, whipping cream, and vanilla extract into the small can. Put the lid on the small can and tape it shut so that it won't fall off. Place the small can inside the larger can. Surround the small can with alternating layers of packed ice and salt. Pour the water over the ice and salt mixture. Put the lid on the large can and tape it shut so that it won't fall off. Now kick the can back and forth so that the ingredients inside get all mixed up! When you get tired, pull out the small can and shake it around. Your Kick the Can Ice Cream is done when the ice cream inside holds together. Grab some spoons and share it right out of the can.

ICE CREAM ON THE WEB

Here's a fun Web site that centers round the tastiest ice cream we know . . . Ben and Jerry's: www.benjerry.com

Friendship from Afar

It's hard to say goodbye to a friend, whether it's after a summer at camp or at the end of the school year, or worst of all, if your friend is moving to another town. However, there are lots of ways to keep in touch these days. You can always pick up the phone or send your pal an E-mail, but we still like the old-fashioned method of good old, write-it-yourself, lick-it-up-and-stamp-it letter-writing!

You can keep in touch with this handy traveling journal. You and your friend will need to buy one journal to send back and forth to each other. You can find blank journals at book or stationery stores. Fill it up with your ideas, stories, and mementos. Then you won't feel like you're so far away!

A traveling journal is the perfect place for including funny notes, photographs, artwork, or anything else that will let a friend know you're thinking of them. Send your friend a program from your school play or ticket stubs from a movie you have seen (complete with your very own review). Draw pictures, make up jokes, ask questions, play a game of tic-tac-toe (OK, a really slow game), or ponder the big questions of life. Just make the journal a special connection between two friends. It can bridge the distance between you and make opening your mail much more fun!

> **She'll wish there was more, and that's the great art o' letter-writin'.**
>
> — FROM *THE PICKWICK PAPERS* BY CHARLES DICKENS

Fall

Autumn leaves are falling down,
Back to school and
Friends abound!
Book group buddies and
Groovy shoes,
Dump chili in a pot or
Be spooky if you choose!
Crisp, sweet apples
And a nip in the air,
Everlasting friendships
And fall fun everywhere!

Fall Apple Fizzies

Fall is one of our favorite seasons. We love seeing amber and auburn leaves filtering golden sunlight, and ripe pumpkins and apples ready for harvest. We understand that you might be a little bummed out to see summer pass, but fall can be just as much of a blast! Look in the newspaper and try to find an apple orchard where you can pick apples. Or pick out some juicy Red Delicious apples at the market for this next project.

For two Fizzies, you will need
- 2 big, clean apples
- Paring knife
- 2 cups cold raspberry ginger ale
- Straws for sipping

Place the apples on a cutting board. Ask an adult to help you core the apples and carve out a large hole in the center of each one. Be careful not to poke all the way through the apple or it will leak. Chop up this part of the apple into tiny bits. Immediately pour raspberry ginger ale into the hollowed-out apples. Add the chopped apple bits. Slide in a couple of straws and slowly sip your Apple Fizzies.

Fallen Leaf Fort

If you have an abundance of fallen autumn leaves around your yard, consider building a Fallen Leaf Fort. After an active autumn day, it's a great place to unwind with a friend.

You will need to make a form with about 20 feet of chicken wire. Always use garden gloves when cutting the wire! Bend the wire to make a circular form, much like a corral. Your fort should be no taller than waist high so that you can climb into it. Use string to tie and connect the edges of the wire as illustrated. Rake a large pile of dry leaves. Begin covering the outside of the form by piling leaves around the base. Pile them all the way to the top of the form. If there are still uncovered spots, take handfuls of leaves and poke them through the holes of the chicken wire until your fort is very leafy and very private.

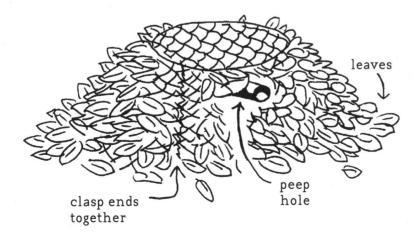

leaves

clasp ends together

peep hole

Candy Cones

Beat the first-day-of-school-blues! You may have mixed emotions about the first day of school. You've had a great summer spending time outdoors with your friends and you'll miss those long summer nights. But you're also eager to get back into the swing of things. In Germany, students exchange paper cones filled with candy and cookies in order to cheer up their friends on the first day back. This could be a great new tradition to start at your school!

You will need
- Ruler
- Pencil
- White or colored poster board
- Scissors
- Markers (optional)
- Tape
- Small beads, sequins, or rhinestones
- Rubber cement
- Hole punch
- Ribbon
- Colored tissue paper

To make the cone, use your ruler and a pencil to outline an 11-by-11-inch square on the poster board. Draw a curved line from one corner to the opposite corner. Cut along that line. (If you'd like to color the cone with markers, go ahead and do so before rolling the paper.) Roll the poster board so that the two straight edges overlap by several inches. Tape the two edges together all along the seam.

You can finish off the cones by gluing tiny beads, sequins, and rhinestones all over the outside of the cone. Allow the cone to dry and then punch holes on either side of the top. Thread the ribbon through and tie a knot on each side. Fill with colored tissue paper and your friend's favorite treats!

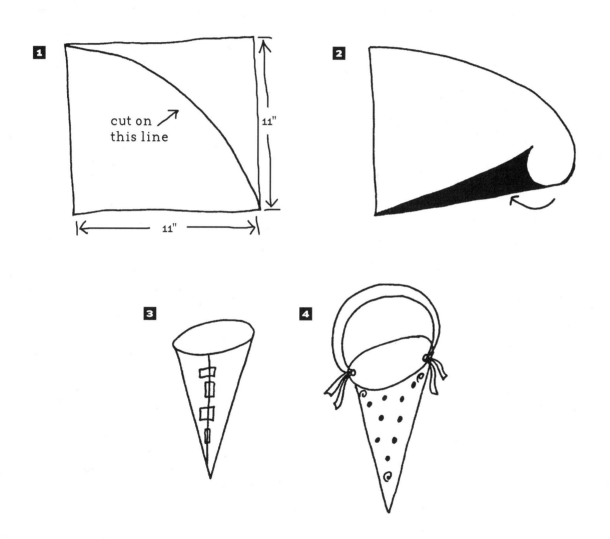

1 cut on this line 11" 11"

2

3

4

Locker Shocker

Surprise your friend with a special locker decorated just for her. It's a great way to welcome her back to school! Be sure to get to school early so that you'll have enough time to decorate in secret.

Cover the locker with colored paper, balloons, glitter, crepe paper, or pictures. Or think of the things that your friend likes and make a collage to cover the entire door. To let her know who created this fantastic display, enlarge a picture of yourself on a copy machine and write a hello message stemming from your mouth. As the last hurrah, write messages on sticky notes and place them in your friend's notebooks to keep her laughing throughout the day.

Ideas for the inside
- Candy tied to ribbons
- Balloons
- Photos from summer
- Words cut out of magazines that describe your friend
- Pictures of her favorite movie stars
- Poem or letter: an ode to friendship

Ideas for the outside
- Cut out her name from construction paper and then cover with glitter
- Create a message with magazine letters
- Crepe paper, ribbon, or balloons
- Cover her locker in colored construction paper and ask all of your friends to write a special note

Book Group Buddies

If you and your friends love to read, then a book group may be exactly what you're looking for. The term "book group"came about when people started getting together to talk about the interesting stories they were reading. Book groups are great because they get you thinking about the books you love—and introduce you to books that you might not have picked up on your own. Here are some general guidelines for your book group.

Choose your group
The group can be as few as two, or as large as ten. Meetings can be held once a month or once week—it's all up to you.

Choose your book
Choosing which book to read next is quite fun—and sometimes quite challenging. Depending on the size and nature of your group, you can either make the choice together or have a different person choose at each meeting. If you need help finding good books, ask your librarian or local bookstore for recommendations.

You can also check out this Web site which features children's literature recommendations: www. parentsplace.com.

Read your book
Everyone should finish the book before the meeting so that you can all discuss the story. The discussion can cover any or all parts of the book. What happened in the story? Why did the main characters do what they did? How did the story make you feel? What was your favorite part of the book? If you could rewrite the ending, how would you change it?

Enjoy!

Remember to have fun! You may disagree with another member regarding your feelings about the book—but you can agree to disagree. That's why books are great. They allow us to learn about other cultures, worlds, and people and they impact each of us in a different way.

Every book group meeting needs snacks! Have everyone bring some snacks to share. And you can make Book Lover's Tea to sip on.

Book Lover's Tea

- Packet of presweetened instant iced tea
- Packet of presweetened instant lemonade
- Water
- 2 pitchers
- Mixing spoon
- Drinking glasses
- Cinnamon sticks
- Candy red hots

In one of the pitchers, prepare the instant iced tea as directed on the package. In the other pitcher, prepare the instant lemonade as directed on the package. Mix each pitcher thoroughly. In each glass, pour one half tea and one half lemonade. You can choose to serve your tea hot or cold. To warm up the tea, place the glasses in the microwave for 20 to 30 seconds. Then garnish with a cinnamon stick and a few candy red hots.

OUR FAVORITE BOOKS

Letters from Rifka
by Karen Hesse

Sarah, Plain and Tall
by Patricia MacLachlan

National Velvet
by Enid Bagnold

The Wind in the Willows
by Kenneth Grahame

Mrs. Frisby and the Rats of Nimh
by Robert C. O'Brien

One-Eyed Cat by Paula Fox

Little House on the Prairie
by Laura Ingalls Wilder

The Hobbit by J. R. R. Tolkien

The Giver by Lois Lowry

The Chronicles of Narnia
by C. S. Lewis

A Wrinkle in Time
by Madeleine L'Engle

Little Women by Louisa May Alcott

Old Yeller by Fred Gipson

From your parents you learn love and laughter and how to put one foot in front of the other. But when books are opened you discover that you have wings.

—HELEN HAYES

Dried Flower Bookmark

If you're an avid reader, you'll need a few pretty bookmarks! These floral beauties will keep you thinking warm thoughts while you're wrapped up in a cozy blanket reading a favorite story.

Harvest flower blossoms and bits of greenery in early fall while the flowers are still in bloom. This project requires a few weeks for the drying process—but after you've waited patiently for the flowers to dry, you'll be rewarded with beautiful keepsakes that preserve the season's color.

You will need
- Freshly picked flowers
- Old telephone book
- Pencil
- Ruler
- Construction paper
- Small, pointed paintbrush
- White glue
- Crayons or markers
- Clear contact paper
- Scissors

Begin by searching for your favorite flowers. Flat flowers such as daisies, geraniums, and pansies work best because they press easily. Stems and leaves are very pretty too. Place the flowers between the pages of an old telephone book and add extra weight to the top of the book (two heavy books work well). Inspect the flowers each week, but leave the flowers to dry for a total of four to six weeks.

contact paper
goes over bookmark

When your flowers are completely flat and thoroughly dry you are ready to create! Use your pencil and ruler to outline your bookmark on construction paper. A traditional rectangular shape works nicely but you can choose any shape or size. (Do not cut the bookmark out until the very end.) Lay your pressed flowers and leaves on the construction paper tag in a pattern you like. Use the dry paintbrush to move them carefully, for they are very delicate and may tear.

Once you have placed the flowers in your chosen pattern, pick up one flower at a time and use the paintbrush to put a little glue on the back. Then put the flower into position. Use your crayons or markers to decorate around the flowers if you'd like. Cut out a piece of contact paper larger than the outline of the bookmark. Peel off the backing and smooth the sticky side of the contact paper onto the bookmark from one end to the other. Cut out the bookmark and "voila!" You're ready to read!

cut
bookmark
out

A book is like a garden carried in the pocket.

—CHINESE PROVERB

Volunteer Project: Keep America Beautiful!

When you're riding your bike, taking a walk, or driving along in the car, take a good, long look at the litter that surrounds you. Unfortunately, you'll find it everywhere. Empty pop cans, fast food containers, paper, paper, and more paper. You and a friend can help to keep litter at bay by having weekly or monthly "cleanup walks." Simply grab a couple of garbage bags and hit the sidewalk, picking up scraps of litter wherever you find it. (If you'd like, wear plastic gloves to keep your hands clean.) Use one bag for paper and the other for cans and glass. This way you can recycle all of it when you get home.

It is crucial that we keep the land that surrounds us as clean as we possibly can. Recycling has helped reduce the amount of garbage that ends up in our overused landfills. It allows us to reuse materials, while saving natural resources for everyone. When you've finished your cleanup walk, take a few moments to enjoy the beautiful outdoors. This next activity is for the tree hugger in all of us.

KIDS FOR A CLEAN ENVIRONMENT

A nine-year-old girl started Kids for a Clean Environment (Kids F.A.C.E.®). You can contact the group on the Internet at www.kidsface.org. By becoming a member (it's free), you can get some great ideas on how kids can really make a difference for the environment.

Hug a Tree

All you need is a friend, a blindfold, and a nice group of trees. Blindfold your friend and guide her to a tree trunk. Let her run her hands up and down the tree's bark, feeling for distinguishing characteristics (knobs, stubs, and areas of smooth bark). Help her hug the tree to feel how large it is in her arms. Help her step around the tree to feel the crunch of leaves or pine needles under her feet. Then just let her listen to the life around the tree—the birds that sit in the tree's branches, the wind that whistles through its leaves. Move her back to the original starting point and remove her blindfold. Your friend can then hug as many trees as necessary until she finds her own!

TIME IT TAKES FOR LITTER TO DISINTEGRATE

Paper gum wrapper: 2 to 4 weeks

Banana peel: 3 to 5 weeks

Cigarette filter: 2 to 5 years

Plastic container: 20 to 30 years

Rubber tire: 50 to 80 years

Aluminum can: 200 to 400 years

Glass bottle: up to 1,000 years

THINGS TO DO ON A BEAUTIFUL AUTUMN DAY

Jump in a big pile of leaves

Visit an apple orchard

Talk a long walk through fall foliage

Pick a pumpkin from a patch

Stuff a scarecrow

Picnic under a colorful tree

Build a leaf fort

Toss a football

Go on a hay ride

Decorate a gourd

Terra-cotta Pebble Pot

We made our first Pebble Pot after strolling along the Wisconsin shores of beautiful Lake Superior one autumn day. We collected so many pretty pebbles and rocks that we had to come up with some way to use them. These pots are a great way to display a collection. They make spectacular gifts, too!

For one Pebble Pot, you will need
- Newspapers
- Popsicle stick
- Terra-cotta flowerpot, any size
- Brown or white tile adhesive (from a hardware store)
- Handfuls of pretty pebbles (enough to cover the outside of your pot)
- Spray shellac

Put several sheets of newspaper down to protect the floor. Using a popsicle stick, carefully cover the outside of the pot with a thick layer of tile adhesive. (Watch out! This stuff is sticky!) Quickly push the pebbles into the adhesive. You may choose to stick them very close together, in a pattern, or with a little bit of space in between the pebbles. Try to vary the sizes and colors for an interesting effect. Allow your Pebble Pot to dry. This could take up to a week if the weather is humid. Check your pot daily by giving a couple of pebbles a gentle pull. When they are set, you will not be able to wiggle them. Over time, the adhesive will become rock hard.

Spread more newspapers on the ground and place your pot in the middle. It is best to do this outside! With the help of an adult, spray a little shellac onto your pot. This will make the pebbles look wet and shiny. You may choose to add some potting soil and a nice plant to your beautiful Pebble Pot.

Getting-to-Know-You Games

You've probably got lots of different kinds of friends. There are the friends you've known for a long time, the ones who know you so well that they can read your feelings like an open book. There are the friends with whom you have fun on sports teams or while you're away at camp. And then there are new friends—new kids who have joined your class or moved in around the corner! When you feel like getting to know people better, games are a great way to break the ice.

Ice Breaker

You'll need lots of balloons and pieces of paper for this game of mini-charades. Before your guests arrive, write out a list of people, animals, places, events, or objects that can be "acted out" by your guests. You might want to choose a theme to make it easier. If this is your soccer team, you could pick out all soccer-related objects and phrases. Tear the list into individual "actions" and place each slip inside of a balloon before you blow it up. When you're ready to play, just ask each guest to select a balloon, pop it, and act out what is written on the paper. All the

rest should guess. Keep going around until you run out of balloons!

The Question Game

The object of this game is to learn more about the feelings, thoughts, and emotions of the people playing. It is important that everyone answers truthfully and respects the feelings of all in the group. Before the game begins, take some time to think about questions that will get your group talking. Start out with easier questions such as "What was your favorite toy when you were little?", "What is your very first memory?",

"Who would you become if you could go back in time?", "If you could travel anywhere in the world, where would you go?", or "What is your most embarrassing moment?"

Then move on to more thought-provoking questions such as "If you could change one thing about your personality, what would it be?", "Which person in your life has had the most impact on you?", "If your house was burning down and you could grab only one possession (all people and animals are safe), what would it be?", "What is the most important ingredient in a good friendship?", or "What is the kindest thing you have ever done for someone else?" Have fun taking turns asking and answering questions that will really get you talking.

Sit On It!

You'll need at least six people for this game, which is based on trust and teamwork. Ask everyone to form a circle, standing shoulder to shoulder. On the count of three have everyone turn to their left and slowly sit down at the same time on the lap of the person behind them. See how long you can keep this sitting circle in tact.

Story Stumper

This game is best for a large group of people. Divide the group into three teams of three or more. Each team should go somewhere they can talk privately. Each team member should share a funny story about themselves—anything from an embarrassing moment to a momentous occasion. After each member has had a chance to share, decide as a group on the "best" story of the bunch. All teams should return to the playing area and one team will go first. Each member of the team will tell a different part of the story, acting as if it really happened to them. The whole group then guesses which team member's story it really is!

Each friend represents a world in us, a world possibly not born until they arrive, and it is only by this meeting that a new world is born.

—ANAIS NIN

Groovy Two Shoes

Save this activity for a day when you and your friends want to spice up your wardrobe! All of you should dig through your closets and find an old pair of canvas tennis shoes. (White works best, but any color will do.) These colorful shoes will add a real kick to your step.

You will need
- Canvas tennis shoes, a pair from each person
- Pillowcase
- Newspaper
- Pencil
- Fabric paint and paintbrush or fabric markers (from a craft store)
- Fabric glue (from a craft store)
- Glitter
- New shoelaces, a pair for each person

For best results, ask everyone to give their tennies a good scrub before coming over to paint. Let the shoes dry completely. When the shoes are ready to be decorated, have each person tie together the laces of their shoes and throw them into the pillowcase. One by one, each girl will close her eyes and pick a pair of shoes from the pillow-case. If you pick your own shoes, pick again. Match the shoes to their owner and paint her tennies!

Cover the floor or table with newspaper. Then go crazy with design and color! Draw your design on the shoe, in pencil. Use the shape of the shoe to provide background (such as flower petals around each of the lace holes). Fill in the outlines with fabric paint or markers. Use the glue to add glitter designs. Paint the new laces with a matching design (hint: a pencil eraser dipped in paint makes great polka dots). Wait overnight for the shoes and laces to dry. Thread them up and present your friend with her cool new shoes.

Autumn Friendship Journal

Creating and writing in journals is an expression of yourself! If you share your journal entries with a friend, you can open up a whole new world of conversation.

You will need
- Colorful fall leaves
- Glue
- Piece of construction paper (8½ by 11 inches)
- Markers
- Scissors
- Clear contact paper
- 20 to 25 sheets of white paper (8½ by 11 inches)
- Hole punch
- Ribbon or string

First, make sure your leaves are dry and flat—you might want to press them flat under a heavy book before beginning. In order to make your journal cover, simply place a small outline of glue on the back of each leaf and apply it to a piece of colored construction paper. Use the markers to decorate around the leaves and to write the title of your journal. Now remove the backing from a sheet of contact paper that is larger than your cover and smooth the sticky side of the contact paper on top of the leaves. Press well and cut away the excess edges for a perfect fit. Stack the white paper neatly and place your decorated cover on top. Punch four holes down the left-hand side of the journal and string the ribbon through to keep the pages in place. Now you're ready to write!

The first rule of journal writing is that privacy is important. Each person needs to understand that her journal is her own, to be shared when she chooses. Here are some fun ideas for journal writing and sharing:

Chronicle Events of the Day

Pretend you are investigative journalists recording the events around you each day. Journalists look for the answers to six main questions: Who, What, When, Where, Why, and How? You can look for the answers to these questions too as you write stories about your neighborhood, family, school, or anything else that interests you! Read your stories aloud to one another or put them together in the form of your very own newspaper!

Record History

Interview special people—grandparents, parents, and aunts and uncles—to record your family history. Ask them questions about their childhood (what is your fondest memory?), their teenage years (how were things different when you grew up?) and the early days of marriage (how did you meet Grandpa?). You'll learn a lot about people you love and your family will treasure the memories you capture.

The Thankful List

Each day, take a few moments to think about what meant the most to you that day. Write down five to ten things that you are grateful for—anything can be included, from your comfortable bed to a special friend. Share these entries with each other and you will realize how lucky you are!

Friend Profile

Set up an interview and ask your friend questions about her family, favorite activities, special memories, feelings, and interests. Pretend as if you know nothing about her as you pull together your list of questions.

contact paper over cover

stack, cut and tie

Migajon

Migajon (mee-gah-HONE) is a claylike substance that Central and South Americans use to make tiny toys and figurines. It is made with a couple of common household ingredients that usually are not paired together in recipes! Mixing glue and white bread makes an excellent moldable dough for making all sorts of neat things like little people and animals, beads, decorations, doll dishes, and charms.

You will need
- 4 slices of white bread
- 4 tablespoons white glue
- Food coloring
- Knife
- Bowl
- Measuring spoons
- Acrylic paint (optional)

Cut the crust off the bread. Rip the bread into little bits. Using your hands, mix the glue with the bits of bread to make supersticky dough. Keep mixing until it is smooth and claylike. Divide the dough and mix in a few drops of food coloring to each part. Use small blobs of dough to form whatever you like. Let the figures harden in a warm, dry spot. You may also paint your hardened figures.

Mini Birthday God's Eyes

How do you help a friend celebrate her birthday? Ask all of her friends to come together and make **Mini Birthday God's Eyes**—one for every year of her life! When she's wearing these colorful little creations around school, everyone will know to wish her a happy day.

You will need
- Colored toothpicks
- Embroidery thread in a few different colors
- Scissors
- Beads

1. Place two colored toothpicks in one hand and place them on top of one another in the form of a cross (+) between your thumb and forefinger. Choose the color of embroidery thread that you'd like to start with and use your free hand to begin wrapping the thread diagonally where the two toothpicks cross. Wrap in this diagonal direction about 10 times. Then switch directions so you are wrapping the thread to form an X in the other diagonal direction. Wrap again about 10 times.

2. Now pull the thread away and wrap it under and around one of the toothpicks. Move the thread to the next toothpick on the left and wrap the thread under and around that toothpick. Again, move the thread to the next toothpick to the left and wrap the thread under and around. Continue threading the toothpicks under and around, moving counterclockwise around the cross sign. As you move, keep your thread flat and smooth so that each layer of thread moves farther out toward the edges.

3. When you are ready to switch thread colors, cut the thread you are using and tie it

in a knot to the end of your new colored thread (snip off the extra thread just at the knot to keep it clean looking). Continue threading under and around in a clockwise fashion and switching colors as often as you'd like. When you have completed weaving the God's Eye, simply cut the

hread and tuck it into the back of the God's Eye.

4. Form a chain of Mini Birthday God's Eyes with embroidery thread and beads and attach them to the belt of the birthday girl. Or tie them to her locker, desk, or backpack!

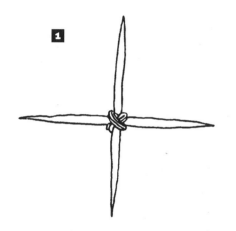

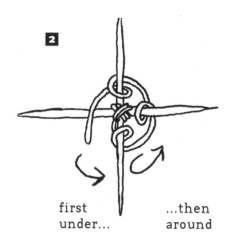

first under...   ...then around

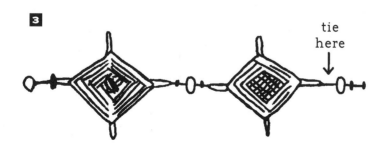

tie here

Halloween Party

Howls and groans and creaks and moans. That's what makes Halloween such a riot. And such a perfect occasion for throwing a bash! Although the tradition of Halloween was then thousands of years old and celebrated throughout the world, it was not widely celebrated in the early days of the United States. Colonists did enjoy Mischief Night, which was an evening of harmless pranks, hayrides, storytelling, and bobbing for apples. In the 1800s, many Irish and Scottish immigrants arrived in America and brought with them a more modern Halloween celebration. Americans began carving pumpkins, visiting homes, and offering prayers for the dead in exchange for gifts of food, parading to scare away evil spirits, and having harvest parties.

You can continue this ancient tradition when you throw a Halloween party! Be creative when you're setting the mood—toss around some spider webs, screw in black light bulbs, turn up a scary sound effects tape, and gather spine tingling ghost stories to share. Invite guests who aren't easily spooked, and make sure that they come dressed in costume!

Boo Brew

This shocking punch will be a hit at the party! As if the floating ghosts weren't enough, the melting sherbet adds a mysterious mist of ghoulishness.

You will need

- Jug of shocking green or shocking blue premixed fruit drink (like Hi-C)
- 2 to 3 pears (firm, and not too ripe)

- Knife
- Scissors
- Toothpick
- Blue food coloring
- Small bowl
- Lemon juice
- Ziplock baggie
- Punch bowl
- 2 liter bottle of lemon seltzer water
- Small carton of lemon or lime sherbet

Put the jug of fruit drink in the refrigerator to chill. Ask an adult to help you cut very thin pear slices. Using the scissors, carefully cut ghost shapes out of the pear slices. You can poke holes with the toothpick (dipped in blue food coloring) for eyes and mouths. Soak the "ghosts" in a small bowl of lemon juice. (This will prevent them from turning brown.) Place them in a Ziplock baggie and set aside. When the party is ready to begin, pour the fruit drink into the punch bowl and add the lemon seltzer water. Plop in some large scoops of sherbet and swirl it around a bit. Float the "ghosts" in the punch. Spooky!

Halloweenies

What does a ghost eat for dinner? Why, Halloweenies of course! There'll be no moaning and groaning when you serve these creepy dogs—just shrieks of approval!

Makes 16 servings

You will need
- Package of 8 refrigerator crescent rolls
- Package of small cocktail wieners
- Baking sheet
- Black food coloring paste (from a party or craft store)
- New, thin paintbrush
- Spatula
- Ketchup
- Mustard
- Fork

Preheat the oven to 375 degrees. Be sure to ask an adult for permission before using the oven. Separate the crescent roll dough into eight triangles. Cut each triangle in half so that you have two smaller triangles that are the same size. Place each wiener at the wide end of a dough triangle and roll them up. Place the rolled up wieners on an ungreased baking sheet. Using the black food coloring paste and a thin paintbrush, paint a dark black spider on each Halloweenie. Bake for about 10 minutes, or until the dough has lightly browned. Serve hot! Mix an orange dipping sauce by combining one part ketchup to two parts mustard.

Wicked Winks

For this game, you need at least six players, but the more the merrier—or shall we say, scarier? Turn the lights low and have the players sit in a circle with their eyes closed. A nonplayer (like a little brother or an adult) secretly chooses the first Winker. Players open their eyes, but do not speak. Everyone glances at the faces about the circle. When the Winker makes eye contact with a player, and feels that she can make her move without being seen by the others, she quickly winks. Her "victim" waits three seconds (so that she doesn't give the Winker's secret identity away) and then states, "I'm out!" and leaves the game. The game continues and the remaining players try to guess the identity of the Winker. A player who guesses incorrectly is out. The player who guesses correctly is the winner!

Ghost in the Graveyard

The best place to play this active outdoor game is in your yard. One person is selected to be the first ghost. She retreats to the backyard to hide in the "graveyard." The remaining players wait at a designated "home base" in the front yard. They begin counting slowly from one o'clock to midnight. At midnight, the group sets off for the graveyard. Their mission? To venture through the graveyard and back to home base without getting tagged by a ghost. Once they have entered the graveyard, the group may split up but may not turn back! No matter how spooky it gets, the only way to get back to the safety of home base is to run through the entire graveyard (around the house). Tagged players are whisked off into the spirit world and become ghosts in the next round. The game is over when the last player is tagged.

DYNAMIC DUOS

It's Halloween and you and your buddy haven't got a thing to wear? Why not rummage through the closets and dress as one of these dynamic duos?

Skipper and Gilligan

Winnie-the-Pooh and Piglet

Abbott and Costello

Raggedy Ann and Andy

Laurel and Hardy

Snoopy and Woodstock

Mickey Mouse and Minnie Mouse

Autumn Twinklers

Pretty pierced lanterns like these are made in Spain! Two friends can work together to punch holes in the tin can Twinklers. When you're done, place them where you want to add a little sparkle.

For two Twinklers, you will need
- 2 empty tin cans with lids off
- Water
- Markers
- Towel
- Thick nail
- Hammer
- 2 votive candles

Wash out the cans and peel off the labels. Fill them with water and put them in the freezer to freeze solid. Draw a dot design on the can with markers. Lay one frozen can on its side on top of a folded towel. With a hammer, carefully pound the nail into the side of the can with a hammer following the pattern of dots. Take turns holding each other's cans while pounding away. Be careful not to smash any fingers! Punch holes all over the cans by pounding the nail, pulling it out, and then pounding another hole. When you are both happy with your patterns of holes, put the cans in the sink to let the water drain out. Place a votive candle in the bottom of each Twinkler and ask for help lighting it. Find a spot to admire each other's Autumn Twinklers.

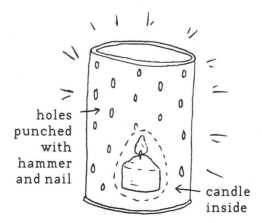

holes punched with hammer and nail

candle inside

Old-Time Radio Show

Can you imagine a world without home computers, CD boom boxes, and televisions? In the 1940s, American families gathered together in front of a radio to listen to their favorite shows. There were love stories, dramas, and mysteries that captured the attention of these families with intriguing story lines, colorful characters, and fantastic sound effects. After all, there was no picture to stare at, so the creators of the radio shows had to be very imaginative! You and your friend can produce an old-time radio show. It's a lot of fun and you can share your finished product with your families or other friends.

You will need
- Cassette tape player or boom box
- Blank cassette tape (or one that you can tape over)
- Access to materials for sound effects

The Script
You may either write a script or use a published piece of work. If you choose to write your own script, you can use the guidelines below to get started.

The Story Line
What kind of story will you write?
- Love story
- Realistic fiction
- Mystery
- Drama
- Western
- Fantasy
- Historical fiction
- Comedy
- Spooky story
- Science fiction

The Action

What is the action in your story? A good story has a problem and a solution theme. Here's a hint: you may want to pick some interesting characters first, and then decide what kind of problem they face in your story.

The Characters

Who are the main characters in your story? Be as creative as you can! You might choose from this list of characters, or invent some of your own.

- Selfish princess
- Lovesick schoolgirl
- Lonesome ghost
- Ingenious detective
- Pioneer farm boy
- Careless cowboy
- Magical fairy
- Misplaced alien

After you have written your script, read through it and make sure you have listed when each character speaks.

The Sound Effects

One of the coolest things about the old-time radio shows was the fantastic sound effects! At which places in your script can you add sound effects? You can always add some good music at the beginning and end of your show, but how about some special effects throughout? Here are some cool sound effects that we like to use: slamming doors, shrieks and hollers, creaky doors, crumpling papers, smoochy kisses, dripping water, rattling pans, barking dogs, and ringing telephones.

Here are ways to create other sound effects:

Horses galloping—clip-clop some empty plastic glasses on a table

Thunderstorms—wiggle a big piece of metal to make a cool stormy rumble

Rain showers—pour some dry beans or popcorn kernels into an empty paper towel roll, tape ends, and shake gently

Breaking glass—pour some silverware into a box and give them one big shake

Footsteps—"walk" shoes (without any feet in them) on a desk or empty box

Collapsing bodies—drop a heavy book onto carpeting for the perfect thud

Crackling fires—slowly crinkle up some cellophane for a really authentic crackle

Rushing streams—turn on a faucet and adjust the water flow. A small, babbling brook will need just a trickle but a roaring river will require a faucet at full-blast!

The Rehearsal

Decide who is going to play each character. Create a different voice for the characters by changing the tone, pitch, speed, and volume of your voices so that the listeners will know which character is speaking. It's fun trying to speak with an accent . . . try it! Practice reading your script a couple of times and practice creating the sound effects. Make sure you know who is responsible for what sound effect!

The Show

It's finally time to tape your Radio Show! When you are ready to begin taping, remember to introduce your Radio Show by announcing the title of the story and its stars. Here's a hint: Learn where your PAUSE button is and use it when you need a break during recording!

The Broadcast

Rewind your Radio Show and enjoy listening to it! If you feel like sharing it, gather an audience, pop some popcorn, and curl up by the "radio" to listen to the captivating sounds of your Old-Time Radio Show.

REAL OLD-TIME RADIO

Before television burst onto the American scene, radio was king! Some of the most popular radio shows in the thirties and forties were adventure programs like *The Shadow*, westerns like *The Lone Ranger*, and comedies like *Ozzie and Harriet* and *Amos and Andy*. *Dragnet* was a favorite adult detective drama, *Superman* was a thriller for kids, and audiences of all ages tuned into *Your Hit Parade* to hear popular music.

Lovin' Spoonfuls

On a cool fall evening, get comfy and settle down for a long girl-to-girl chat with a close friend. Make mugs of hot chocolate and let these delicious candy-coated spoons make the cocoa and the conversation even yummier.

You will need
- 1 cup chocolate, white chocolate, or butterscotch chips
- Small glass bowl
- Metal spoon
- New plastic spoons
- Colored sugars, decorative candies, and sprinkles
- Waxed paper
- Scissors
- Plastic wrap
- Colorful ribbons

Microwave the chips in a glass bowl for about 2 minutes, or until melted. The chips will not appear to be melted, so you will have to stir them with the metal spoon in order to tell. Dip each plastic spoon into the melted chocolate. Cover the spoons with chocolate, but leave the top half of the handle uncoated. Immediately scatter some colorful sugars, decorative candies, or sprinkles onto the spoons. Place the spoons on waxed paper to set. Allow about an hour for the coating to harden completely. Cut small circles or squares from the plastic wrap. Wrap the plastic around a bundle of several spoons, leaving the handles unwrapped. Tie with a pretty ribbon.

don't dip handle!

bowl of melted chocolate chips

chocolate-dipped spoon

South of the Border Friendship Dolls

Picture yourself strolling through an outdoor Guatemalan market. You come across tiny dolls made of wire, bits of brightly colored yarn, and festive scraps of cloth. You've discovered Guatemalan worry dolls! They are so named because children tell their troubles to them before they go to bed and it is believed that the dolls take care of their problems by morning.

South of the Border Friendship Dolls are very similar to worry dolls. You create a tiny doll that looks like you, and a friend makes a different doll in her own likeness. The dolls are exchanged and hung on necklaces. Whenever these necklaces are worn, you'll feel comfort, no worries, and a friend nearby.

For two dolls, you will need
- 2 pieces of pipe cleaner, each 4 inches long
- 2 pieces of pipe cleaner, each 2 inches long
- Embroidery thread (the colors of your favorite clothes and your hair color)
- Scissors
- Glue
- Small beads
- Bits of construction paper
- Colored markers

1. For each doll, fold one of the 4-inch pipe cleaner pieces in half to make the body. Bend each end out for the legs. Give the pipe cleaners a twist about halfway up the body.

2. Twist one of the 2-inch pipe cleaner pieces around the doll's body to make arms.

3. (At this point, remember, you are making a doll that looks like you and your friend is making one that looks like her.) Each of you should think of your favorite pants or jeans and choose the embroidery thread of that color. Tie a piece of thread to the middle of the doll's body with a knot and begin winding the thread down the doll's leg and then back up again. Do the same to the other leg. Cut the thread and glue the end to the back of the doll.

4. Next, each of you should think about your favorite shirt and choose the embroidery thread of that color. Tie a piece of thread to the doll's body with a knot and begin winding the thread along the doll's arm and then back again. Wind the thread around the doll's chest. Move to the other arm and wrap it in the same way. Cut the thread and glue the end to the back of the doll.

5. Using beads or small bits of construction paper, glue hands, feet, and a head onto your doll. With construction paper and markers, draw your face onto your doll. Remember to add the correct eye color!

6. Cut bits of embroidery thread and glue them onto your doll's head for hair. Use construction paper and more thread to make your doll look as much like you as possible.

7. When each of you has created a Friendship Doll in your own likeness, exchange them. Attach the dolls to some embroidery string for a necklace and you'll always have a friend nearby!

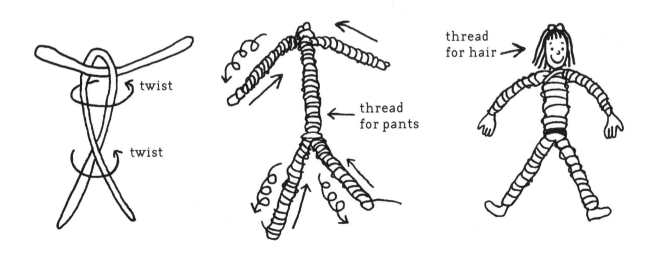

Queen for a Day Coupon Book

In the 1950s, there was a quirky game show on television called Queen for a Day. Contestants competed to launch themselves from their normal humdrum lives to that of a queen. The winner (get a load of this) was the woman who convinced the panel that her life was the most pathetic! Yikes! We know that your lives are anything but boring, so just take this opportunity to give your friend the royal treatment.

If your friend is stressed out by homework, sports, or chores, give her a break. You can make her a coupon book filled with little favors that will make her life a bit easier.

HOW MANY OF THESE POPULAR TV SHOWS FROM THE 1950s AND 1960s DO YOU RECOGNIZE?

I Love Lucy

Lassie

American Bandstand

The Howdy Doody Show

Leave It to Beaver

Gunsmoke

The Mickey Mouse Club

Ozzie and Harriet

You will need
- Scissors
- Construction paper
- Pens or markers
- Hole punch
- Ribbon

Cut your construction paper into five or more pieces of similar size. You can choose a rectangular-shaped coupon or get creative with a heart- or flower-shaped book. Write out and decorate your coupons as you wish. ("This coupon is good for one free back massage" or "This coupon entitles you to one homemade ice cream sundae.") Punch a hole on the left-hand side, string a pretty ribbon through, and tie it in a bow.

Braid It!

If you've ever had a "bad hair" day, you know that sometimes it just feels better to have someone else take care of those fickle strands. With the help of a friend, you can throw caution to the wind and just braid it! We've given you the basics of braiding. If you're beyond the basics, then check out our ideas at the bottom of the page.

It's true that you can simply brush and braid. But when braiding a friend's hair, it's nice to add a few extra special touches. Gently brush her hair out and then give her a little head massage before you begin. Massage her scalp and temples (the area just outside the eye) and let her relax before the braiding begins.

Be sure to brush her hair thoroughly, removing any tangles or knots. Use a wide-toothed comb to divide her hair into three separate but equal sections at the back of her head. Cross the right section over the center section, then cross the left over the new center section. Continue in this way, alternately crossing each outer section over the center section until you run out of hair. The braid will begin to form really quickly. When you finish the braid, tie it with a covered rubber band.

Other Hair Ideas

Create tiny braids all over her head and finish each braid off with a colored rubber band.

Braid each other's hair overnight and wake up in the morning to crazy crimping.

Braid a ribbon into her hair! Tie one end of the ribbon around a ponytail at the top of her hair and then braid it in with a section.

Pull her hair into a ponytail and twist. Knot the twist on top of her head and hold with a chunky clip.

Friendship Frames

They say a picture is worth a thousand words. Photographs remind us of good times and special people and speak volumes about our lives. You and a friend can make a couple of friendship frames and fill them with pictures of you together. You could even make frames for each other!

You will need
- 2 clear acrylic frames
- Newspaper
- Any kind of decorations (bottle caps, coins, buttons, fabric, flowers, shells, or ribbon)
- Glue or rubber cement
- Cotton swabs
- Nail polish remover
- 2 photographs

For each frame, lay the frame on newspaper and then on a flat surface. Make sure the frame is clean and dry. Once you've chosen your decorations, arrange them in a pattern on the frame. Put glue on the back of each piece and affix to the frame. For best results, begin with the bottom row and then move to the sides. Excess glue can be removed with a cotton swab dipped in nail polish remover. Set the frame aside while the glue dries, about an hour or so. Place your photo in the frame and enjoy!

Early American Cornhusk Flowers

The American settlers of long ago had to work with the materials that were available to them. Since running to the nearest toy store for the latest doll or action figure was not an option, many children played with dolls made from cornhusks. The husks are the leaves that surround the ear of corn. In this activity, you will use cornhusks in a way that settlers from long ago may have.

You will need
- Package of liquid synthetic dye
- Bucket
- Dried cornhusks (from craft stores or in the Mexican food section of your grocery store)
- Scissors
- Very thin wire
- Newspapers
- Needle
- Pipe cleaners

The evening before you plan to make the flowers, mix the dye in the bucket according to the directions on the package. Soak the cornhusks in the dye bath for about 12 hours.

The next day, do the following:

1. Cut each cornhusk in half so they resemble two small squares.

2. Stack several wet cornhusks on top of each other.

3. Tightly wrap the wire around the cornhusks at one end of the stack. Cut the wire.

4. Place this bundle on a stack of newspapers. Carefully stick the needle in the cornhusks. Drag the needle through the husks away from you toward the untied end. This will shred the cornhusks, creating "petals."

5. Place the completely shredded bundle on newspapers to dry with the tied end down.

6. When they have dried, wrap a pipe cleaner around the bottom of each flower. Make several of them for an Early American bouquet.

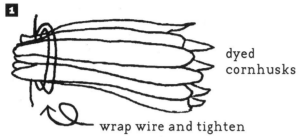

1

dyed cornhusks

wrap wire and tighten

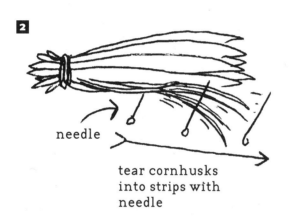

2

needle

tear cornhusks into strips with needle

3

pipe cleaner

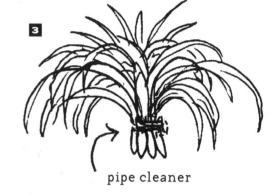

CORN FOR THE AGES

Corn has been growing in the United States for at least 3,000 years! One of the first crops European settlers learned to grow was corn. The settlers used every part of the corn plant to make things. Not only was this versatile plant used for food, but it was also used for things like bedding, corncob pipes, tools, and toys.

Dump-It-in-the-Pot Chili Party

This is a great party idea. First, draw up a guest list. Then divide the list in half. You call half of the guests while your friend calls the other half. Tell the party guests when to come over and ask them to bring one of the ingredients to dump in the pot. Bake a batch of corn bread, rent a good movie, and serve steaming bowls of this tasty chili.

Ask each guest to bring one or two of the following ingredients. The starred items are very important, so make sure that they are included in your chili!

You will need
- Can opener
- Can of chili beans*
- Can of garbanzo beans
- Can of black beans
- Can of corn
- Can of small black olives
- Large can of chopped tomatoes*
- Packet of chili seasoning*
- One pound of cooked ground beef or turkey
- Large pot
- Mixing spoon
- Ladle
- Bowls for chili
- Bag of shredded cheddar cheese (to sprinkle on top!)
- Spoons

When your guests arrive, ask them to dump their undrained ingredients into the pot. Be careful as you warm the chili over medium heat on the stove. Why don't you stir the chili while your friend greets party-goers? Check the consistency of the chili. You may want to add a little water. When the chili begins to bubble, turn off the stove and ladle it into bowls. Sprinkle cheese on top, serve to your guests, and enjoy the delicious results of the cooperative project you and your friend organized.

PIONEER POTLUCK

A potluck is a party where everyone brings something to share. The Dump-it-in-the-Pot Chili Party is a lot like a potluck. You'll never guess who had the first potlucks — the pioneers! After a long day of work, a pioneer family might meet at church or in a town hall and share a dish, conversation, and a little dancing with their neighbors.

Celebrity!

Do you and your friends work as a team? Can you guess what your friends are going to say even before it comes out of their mouths? If you answered "yes" to these questions, then Celebrity will be a fun and exciting game for you and your friends—you can play with as few as four or as many as forty-four! The secret to success is creative thinking and fast talking. Speed is of the essence, but communication is the key!

You will need
- 15 slips of paper per person
- Pens or pencils, 1 for each player
- Hat, bowl, or box (something to pull names from)
- Watch with a second hand

Here's how you play:
1. Give each player fifteen slips of paper and a pen or pencil.

2. Ask each person to think of fifteen famous people and secretly write them down on the slips of paper. (By "famous" we mean anyone from the President of the United States to your local weatherman—it can be anyone in the celebrity spotlight.)

3. Split the group into two equal teams. (Try splitting up by birthdays—January through June on one team and July through December on the other. Or by eye color—blue and green on one side, brown and hazel on the other.)

4. Place all of the slips of paper into the "hat." Flip a coin to determine which team will go first. One member from the first team should volunteer to be the first "reader."

5. The reader then stands up in front of her group and waits for the "go" from the timekeeper (usually a member of the opposite team). The reader will have one

minute to help her team guess as many celebrities as possible. To do this, the reader will select one folded piece of paper from the hat, read it to herself and then begin giving her team verbal clues about the celebrity. She can use any words, phrases, or body language she wants to describe the celebrity, except those that are part of the celebrity's name.

6. Assign a scorekeeper to keep track of correct guesses—one point per correct answer.

Here's an example:
The slip of paper says "Peter Pan." The reader could offer up these clues: "He's a boy who'll never grow up. He lives with his friends in Never-Never Land and loves a girl named Wendy."

The reader will continue with clues until someone on her team yells out the answer. Players on the other team must remain silent at this point. When she hears the correct answer, she'll reach into the hat for another name and start it all again, continuing until one minute is up. If the reader has no idea who the celebrity is, she must get creative. (For example, "His first name is the same as the famous rabbit, (blank) Cottontail. His last name is what we use to cook eggs in, a frying (blank).")

Alternate teams and readers, until each person has had a chance to read. Usually, you will have enough names in the hat to run through the teams twice. If not, add a few more names to the hat. After two full rounds, add up the points and declare the victor!

Winter

Snowflakes tickle
The tip of your tongue,
Swirling snow cream,
Songs are sung.
Celebrate friendship
And a happy New Year,
Make mush, do a dance,
And spread love and cheer.
Winter is such a splendid season—
Hot cocoa, cool parties,
And good friends are the reason!

Fort Frost

If you are lucky enough to live in an area that gets lots of snow, then Fort Frost is for you! It is very easy to make, especially if your friends are there to help you scoop.

Simply make a huge snow mound. Scoop out the inside of the snow mound so that you create a cavity large enough to crawl into. If the cavity is not large enough for you and a friend to share, you can add an "addition" by building another mound next to it and knocking down the connecting snow wall.

3'

dig out
from base
at end

WINTRY THINGS TO DO WITH FRIENDS

Make snow angels

Track animal trails

Toss snowballs

Sled down a hill

Play snow football

Ice skate on a frozen pond

Play frigid frisbee

Build a snowman

Snow Cream

Wait for a perfect, snowy day when the flakes are falling furiously. There should be a layer of snow already covering the ground so that the new snow falls gently on top and stays clean and fresh. Liz used to make Snow Cream with her dad. She would peer out the window, impatiently waiting for the time when just enough fresh snow had fallen. Her dad would pull on his boots and wade through the snow until he found just the right spot to scoop.

You will need
- Big bowl
- Clean, freshly fallen snow
- 1 cup sugar
- 1 tablespoon vanilla extract
- A few drops of food coloring
- ¼ to ½ cup milk

The best place to make Snow Cream is outdoors. Put on mittens and use the big bowl to scoop up a bunch of clean snow. Quickly add the sugar, vanilla extract, and food coloring. Add ¼ cup milk and stir gently. Add more milk if necessary until the mixture is like ice cream. Don't waste any time. Snow Cream waits for no one!

How pretty it is to watch the tiny flakes drift downward in the air as if there were a wedding in the sky and the fairies were throwing confetti.

—CYRIL W. BEAUMONT

Pretzel Wreath for Feathered Friends

This wreath project is for the birds—literally. Your fine-feathered friends will find this wreath irresistible. We're sure that they would thank you for this delicacy if their beaks weren't so busy pecking and nibbling.

You will need
- Coat hanger
- 10 big, hard pretzels
- Pliers
- 3 feet of 16-gauge wire
- Scissors or wire cutters
- Butter knife
- Peanut butter
- Birdseed
- Nut meats
- Raisins
- Dried fruit

1. Ask an adult to help you unravel the twisted part of the coat hanger and bend it into a circle. Thread the pretzels onto the wire as shown in the picture. Twist the ends together with the pliers to close off the wire ring.

2. Cut the 16-gauge wire into ten small pieces. You are going to use these to connect the pretzels together.

3. Twist a piece of wire around a pretzel and then attach it to the pretzel beside it in the same way. Continue to secure all of the pretzels in this manner.

4. Use the knife or your fingers to spread globs of peanut butter onto the pretzel wreath. The peanut butter will act as your glue.

5. Press birdseed, nuts, raisins, and other dried bits of fruit into the peanut butter globs.

6. Use an additional long piece of wire to attach the wreath to a tree. Twist the wire around some of the pretzels and then wrap it around the trunk.

7. Give the birds a couple of days to find your wreath. Once they do, they'll visit often!

FEED THE BIRDS

Birds are hungry all the time! Would you like to know who eats what? Cardinals and sparrows like sunflower seeds and robins rave about raisins and fruit. Mockingbirds and doves enjoy eating fruit, too. Finches find corn and nuts to be quite delicious, as do mourning doves and blue jays. Red-bellied woodpeckers love cracked corn, while yellow-bellied sapsuckers crave mixtures of fruit and nuts. Peanut butter, whether creamy or crunchy, is always a crowd pleaser! If you would like more information about birds, write to: The National Audubon Society, 645 Pennsylvania Ave., SE, Washington, DC 20003.

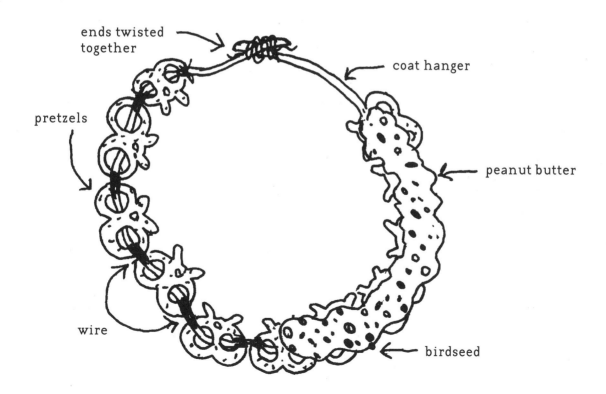

ends twisted together

coat hanger

pretzels

peanut butter

wire

birdseed

St. Nicholas Day Surprise

For centuries, people have celebrated St. Nicholas Day on December 6. It began as a European custom and has found its way into many American homes. The real fun begins on December 5, the night before St. Nicholas Day. Children set out their empty shoes at bedtime and in the morning they find them filled with candy and trinkets. Why not adopt this custom and share it with your friend?

Exchange one of your cleanest shoes (save the stinky gym shoes for another activity, please) with each other on December 5. Fill your friend's shoe with her favorite wrapped pieces of candy, stickers, tiny toys, a poem, shiny pennies, a brand new pencil, gingerbread cookies, and other small items that you know she will like. Place the filled shoe outside of your friend's door that evening. Make a pact not to peek at the shoes until morning. On the morning of St. Nick's Day, jump out of bed and race down to find your St. Nicholas Day Surprise waiting for you!

THREE KINGS DAY

Some children celebrate Three Kings' Day on January 6. This celebration honors the story of the three kings who brought gifts to Jesus. The night before Three Kings Day, children set out boxes filled with grass for the kings' camels. In the morning, the grass is gone and in its place are little gifts!

Dipsy Doodles

These chocolate-covered pretzels are a sweet treat to share with your friends and lots of fun to make.

You will need
- 1 bag (16 ounces) chocolate chips
- Small glass bowl
- Metal spoon
- Bag of pretzel rods
- Decorative candies and sprinkles, colored sugars, chopped peanuts, or toffee chips
- Waxed paper
- Aluminum foil (optional)
- Ribbon (optional)

Pour chocolate chips into a small glass bowl and melt them in the microwave for 1 minute. Stir the chips with a spoon and then cook for one more minute. Stir the chips again, and if they are not completely melted, cook for an additional minute. The chips will not appear to be melted, so you will have to stir them in order to tell. Dip half of each pretzel rod into the smooth chocolate and then roll them in sprinkles, sugars, peanuts, or toffee. Place on a sheet of waxed paper and allow them to cool.

Now you have two choices. You may wrap several Dipsy Doodles in aluminum foil, tie with a pretty ribbon, and leave little sweet treats for people you love. Or, you and your friend can gobble them down with a couple of cold glasses of milk. Quite a delicious dilemma, huh?

PRETZEL HISTORY

The first pretzel was made by monks in Europe to reward children who learned their prayers. The traditional pretzel's criss-cross shape represented the crossed arms of a child praying. Many years later, in 1861, the first commercial pretzel bakery opened in the United States in Lititz, Pennsylvania.

Ho Ho Holiday Caroling

Jump into the spirit of the season and sing, sing, sing! Gather your friends together (even those who don't consider themselves "singers") and share a little bit of history by caroling around your neighborhood.

Caroling is one of the oldest customs practiced throughout the world during the Christmas season. You and your friends can continue this wonderful tradition by borrowing songbooks from your music teacher or choir director and taking your voices to the streets! Or simply go door to door singing some of the holiday favorites you know by heart. You will be amazed by the wonderful reaction from your neighbors—nothing is better at holiday time than a merry group of carolers. When you return home, be sure to have some Spiced Hot Chocolate waiting—it's a delicious way to warm up.

Spiced Hot Chocolate

Prepare hot chocolate as directed on the packet. We like using milk instead of water for extra creamy flavor. Add ½ teaspoon cinnamon and ¼ teaspoon nutmeg and top with marshmallows or whipped cream. Add a candy cane for a festive flair.

Cookie Exchange

We love cookie exchanges so much, we have one every year! The magic of this party is that everyone arrives with one kind of cookie and then leaves with a great assortment. Invite friends over and ask them to bring a roll of refrigerated cookie dough, a baking sheet, and a container of frosting or cookie decorations. In order to get a good variety, you might want to ask each friend to bring a certain type of dough and be specific about whether to bring frosting or decorations. Our mouths are watering just thinking about it.

You will need
- Various kinds of refrigerated cookie dough (peanut butter, chocolate, sugar, and chocolate chip)
- Cookie cutters
- Flour (if the dough gets too sticky)
- Baking sheets
- Oven mitt
- Spatula
- Frosting, colored sugars, candy decorations, and sprinkles
- Waxed paper
- Paper plates
- Aluminum foil

Each party guest will work with their own dough. As you sit around talking, each of you will create an interesting and unique batch of cookies. In addition to the assortment of flavors present, you can make the cookies different by the way they are shaped and prepared. Roll some, form some by hand, or cut some out with cookie cutters. Work quickly and keep any dough you are not working with in the refrigerator so that it does not get sticky. If it does, sprinkle a little flour on your hands and on the work space. When a particular batch of cookies is ready, place it on an ungreased baking sheet. Bake the batch according to the directions on the package. Ask an adult for help while using the oven, and always use an oven mitt.

When the cookies are cool, use frosting, sugars, candy decorations, and sprinkles to decorate them. After decorating, lay all the cookies on sheets of waxed paper. With a paper plate in hand, take turns selecting cookies until all of them are gone. Wrap the plates in aluminum foil. Take your assortment of cookies home and share them with your family, neighbors, or other friends!

Season of Celebrations

December is an active month filled with many meaningful and festive celebrations! December brings Hanukkah, the ancient eight-day Festival of Lights. On the 25th, people celebrate Christmas. December 26 marks the first day of Kwanzaa. No matter what you and your family celebrate, it is interesting to learn about the beliefs and customs of others. Enjoy this spirited month and honor these important traditions by giving these activities a try.

Hanukkah: The Dreidel Game

Hanukkah is the Hebrew word for "dedication." It is a Jewish holiday celebrating great miracles that happened long ago. Families observe Hanukkah by lighting the candles on a menorah each of the eight nights, singing songs, and exchanging gifts between loved ones. Children eat delicious potato pancakes and enjoy playing a game with a top called a dreidel.

Before they were manufactured, children spent weeks carving dreidels out of wood.

These dreidels are much easier to make and will do the trick!

You will need
- Cardboard, 3 inches square
- Ruler
- Scissors
- Pencil
- Marker
- Long, thick nail
- Pennies, candy, nuts, or raisins

Take your 3-inch-square piece of cardboard and use a ruler to draw a diagonal line from one corner of the square to the other.

Draw another diagonal line so that you have an X on the square. The X will divide the square into four triangles. A dreidel has a letter on each of its four sides. They stand for the words in the Hebrew sentence "A great miracle happened there." Draw one Hebrew letter in each triangle: Nun, Gimel, Heh, and Shin. Carefully poke the nail through the middle of the square where the lines intersect.

Spinning the Dreidel

Sit in a circle. Each player starts the game with an equal number of pennies, candy, nuts, or raisins. To start, everyone puts five items in the "pot." Players take turns spinning the dreidel like a top. When it stops spinning, look to see what letter is facing up. Here is what each spin means:

Nun	ב	=	do nothing
Gimel	ג	=	take the whole pot
Heh	ה	=	take half of the pot
Shin	ש	=	add one item to the pot

If a player runs out of items, they are out of the game. The player who takes the whole pot (or outlasts everyone else) wins!

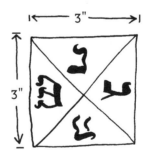

3"

3"

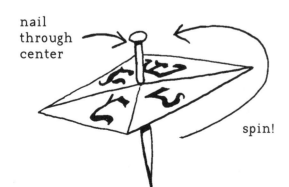

nail through center

spin!

react to this letter

Christmas: Keepsake Ornaments

Christmas is the day that Christians celebrate the birth of Jesus Christ. Families gather to decorate evergreen trees, sing ancient carols, and exchange gifts. A tree ornament is always a thoughtful gift for a friend. Spend some time creating ornaments together and make them really meaningful by adding personal touches, dates, and messages. When hanging ornaments, we are reminded every year of the special friend that gave them to us. There are several ways to make these shiny little balls into beautiful glittering ornaments. Pick your favorite from these tried and true methods.

You will need
- Glass ball ornaments
- Paint pens (silver and gold work well)
- Glue
- Cotton swab
- Glitter
- Sequins and small beads (optional)

You may use paint pens to draw designs onto a glass ball. Try a simple repeated pattern. Allow the paint to dry. Dab little dots of glue around the ornament in a complimentary pattern. Place glitter on the glue dots. When the glue has hardened, write the date with your paint pen.

Another decoration idea is to personalize the ornaments by writing each other's initials (or full names) on the balls with the paint pens. Allow the paint to dry. Swirl a little glue around the monogram. A cotton swab makes a nice tool—it spreads the glue in an interesting way. Sprinkle glitter onto the glue for a lovely effect. Add sequins and small beads, if you like.

Kwanzaa: Woven Mkeka

Many African Americans celebrate their heritage during Kwanzaa. Families gather together on each of the celebration's seven nights, light a candle on the kinara (candle holder), and discuss the ideals that will strengthen family and community. The seven principles of Kwanzaa are unity, self-determination, collective work and responsibility, cooperative economics, purpose, creativity, and faith.

Kwanzaa symbols are placed on a mat called a mkeka. Throughout the week, the mat will hold a bowl of fruit and vegetables, ears of corn, the kinara, a unity cup, literature, and African art. You and a friend can weave a *mkeka* incorporating the three colors of Kwanzaa—red, black, and green. Red yarn represents the struggle for freedom, black yarn represents the unification of black people, and green yarn represents the future.

For one Mkeka, you will need
- Pencil
- 9-inch paper plate
- Ruler
- Scissors
- Green yarn
- Black yarn
- Red yarn
- Tape

1. With your pencil draw a circle the size of a half-dollar in the center of the paper plate. Then, using your pencil and ruler, divide the plate into nine wedges.

2. Cut along the lines until you reach the center circle and stop there. Flip the plate over. Tape the end of one long piece of yarn near the center of the back of the plate. Beginning at the center of the plate, weave the yarn over and under the wedges. Weave until you reach the end of this piece of yarn. Tape the end to the back of the plate. Tape a new color of yarn to the back of the plate and continue weaving. Repeat this process with the third color of yarn until you reach the outer edge of the plate. Tape the yarn to the back of the plate and snip off any excess.

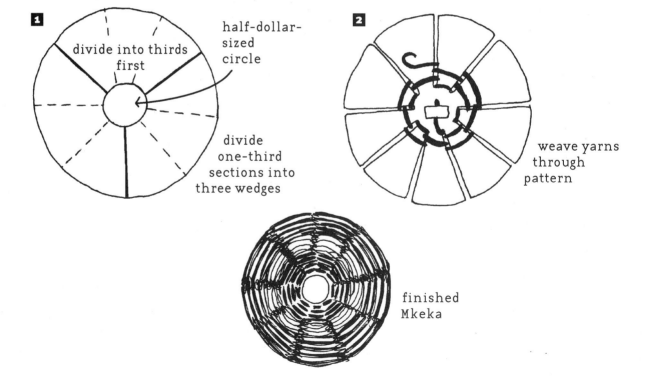

1 half-dollar-sized circle

divide into thirds first

divide one-third sections into three wedges

2 weave yarns through pattern

finished Mkeka

Volunteer Project: Gift Baskets for Older Friends

You have the power to make other people happy—all it takes is a little time and effort. There are people in your community who may be lonely or sad, or who are without the group of friends that you are so lucky to have. This project will give you a reason to bring your friends together and visit a nursing home or elderly neighbor to brighten their day. You may be surprised that when you give of yourself, you'll receive laughter, stories, and fun in return.

You will need
- Baskets (You can buy baskets or make your own "basket" out of anything you can put a handle on and decorate—large tin cans, cardboard boxes, or old Easter baskets)
- Tissue paper or wrapping paper
- Ribbons, bows, and construction paper
- Scissors
- Glue
- Goodies (see the list below for ideas)

For example, you could make a gift basket from an empty coffee can. Just clean the can well and line it with tissue or wrapping paper. Then make a handle out of two pieces of construction paper. Cut long, thick strips and glue them together for a stronger handle. Then glue the ends of the handle to opposite sides of the can and let it dry well. You could cover every inch of the can with bows left over from Christmas and fill it with all sorts of goodies.

Ideas for goodies
- Homemade cookies
- Interesting things to read (books, magazines, or your own stories and poems)
- Picture frames
- Box of tea

- Bookmarks
- Hand lotion
- Candles
- Potpourri

Other ideas for having fun with your older friends

- Put on a mini talent show
- Swap stories
- Sing a song
- Play an instrument
- Play a game of cards
- Tell jokes
- Read a story
- Ask questions to learn what life was like when they were growing up. For example, what is your best memory from childhood? How much did a candy bar cost when you were little? What was your favorite toy? What was school like?

FESTIVAL OF CLEAR BRIGHTNESS

In China children honor their parents, grandparents, and great-grandparents during the Festival of Clear Brightness. Whole families gather to have large picnics and pay tribute to their ancestors. They also clean the gravesites of their ancestors, offering food and flowers as a measure of respect.

For somehow, not only at Christmas,
but all the long year through,
the joy you give to others
is the joy that comes back to you.

—JOHN GREENLEAF WHITTIER

New Year's Traditions

New Year's celebrations evoke a sense of joy and merriment. Different cultures have their own unique calendars; therefore New Year dates differ. For many people around the world, New Year's Eve means staying up late and counting down the seconds to January 1. Americans ring in the New Year with rowdy parties, bubbly drinks, funny hats, horns, noisemakers, and resolutions. Other cultures say goodbye to the old year and celebrate the approach of the new one with their own interesting customs.

Spice up your festivities by adding some of these international traditions to your repertoire. And remember, no matter where you are from or where you are celebrating, it is always important to welcome the new year with someone who is dear to you!

New Year's Eve Traditions Around the World

Spain–When the clock strikes midnight, Spaniards eat twelve grapes for good luck. One grape is eaten on each stroke of midnight. This is an easy tradition to adopt!

Japan–Juicy tangerines symbolizing the sun and steaming bowls of long noodles are eaten at midnight. Red and white are considered lucky colors, so foods of these hues are eaten to bring good luck in the coming year. Think of all the scrumptious "lucky foods" you can enjoy.

Russia–Children wait for Grandfather Frost and the Snow Maiden to visit their homes and leave presents. New Year's Eve is also a time for exchanging greeting cards. Cakes sweetened with honey are baked and eaten during the New Year festivities. Yum!

Germany–In the German state of Bavaria, people count down the seconds to New Year's Eve in the pitch dark. You can imagine the revelry at midnight when the lights go on! In the German Alps, people make as much noise as possible at the onset of the New Year. Blow horns, stomp your feet, toot whistles, and exercise your vocal chords with this spirited tradition!

China–The Chinese New Year starts sometime between late January and early February. It arrives at a different time each year based on the cycles of the moon. The celebration lasts for many weeks for this very important holiday! On New Year's Day, families get dressed up and visit friends. They bring gifts of fruit (oranges are considered lucky), and they eat bowls of noodles that symbolize long life. Children toss firecrackers and a giant dragon leads the New Year's parade. But on the day before that, people gather for delicious New Year's Eve banquets. Adults write poems welcoming the New Year and give children red envelopes with "lucky money" inside.

You can create bright red Lucky Money Envelopes with your friend on New Year's Eve. Why not stuff them with gold foil-wrapped chocolate coins and hand them out to your families and friends on New Year's Day? Use them to wish your loved ones a Happy New Year!

Lucky Money Envelopes

You will need
- Any size envelope
- Pieces of red paper, 8½ by 11 inches
- Pencil
- Scissors
- Glue stick or white glue
- Glitter
- Gold paint pen
- Coins (a lucky penny, silver dollar, or chocolate foil-covered coins)

Pull the envelope apart carefully. Trace the envelope's shape onto the red paper. Cut the traced figure out. Fold the paper the same way as the envelope is folded. Glue the bottom flap to the two side flaps. Decorate the envelope with glitter and add a "Happy New Year" message with the paint pen. Fill the finished red envelope with coins and glue it shut.

GIVE PEAS A CHANCE

Did you know that some Americans honor a Southern tradition and believe eating black-eyed peas on New Year's will bring good luck?

Predicting the Future

What does the New Year have in store for you and your friends? A new acquaintance? An A in Science? In Germany, people pour hot molten lead into icy cold water on New Year's Day. The lead hardens and forms shapes that are examined and used to make predictions for the coming year. If the lead looks like an airplane, perhaps a trip is in the future. If it looks like a coin, maybe great riches are on the way! Let your imagination run wild while predicting your fortunes with this twist on an old German tradition.

You will need
- Thick candle (a votive candle works well)
- Matches
- Bowl of cold water

Get an adult's permission to light the candle. Allow it to burn for several minutes so that melted wax can accumulate near the wick. The person whose future is to be analyzed must blow out the candle and then carefully pour the melted wax into the bowl of cold water. The wax will harden immediately. The prediction maker should scoop out the formation and examine it. What does it look like? Do you see an animal? Maybe your friend will get a new pet this year! Can you make out a heart? Perhaps this could be a year filled with love! Use your imagination, and take turns being the prediction maker. Have fun, and best wishes for a New Year filled with good fortune!

THE NEW YEAR DOESN'T ALWAYS START IN JANUARY

New Year celebrations occur on different days throughout the world. That's because different religions follow different calendars. Sikhs celebrate the New Year in April and Hindus celebrate it in the fall. The Jewish New Year, Rosh Hashanah, comes in September or October.

Wire Charm Bracelets

Funky, chunky jewelry is always in style and these bracelets will reflect your own personal flair. Make the bracelets together as gifts for other girlfriends—or moms, sisters, or aunts too! Half the fun will be traveling to the craft store to find colorful beads, baubles, and pins to create your bracelets.

You will need
- Scissors
- Thin, moldable silver, gold-filled, or brass wire (18-gauge works well)
- Beads of all colors, shapes, and sizes
- Small safety pins (gold and silver)
- Snap swivels or barrel swivels (you can find these cool gold fasteners where you buy fishing gear—or ask your dad if you can rummage through his tackle box!)

Begin by creating your very own wire charms. Use your scissors to cut a short piece of wire and then carefully twist it into whatever shape you'd like! We've made hearts, animals, swirling circles, and all sorts of crazy designs. Thread the beads onto the wire charms for color and texture. Make sure to twist or bend the wire at the ends in order to keep the beads set. Be careful with the sharp ends of the metal wire.

Now you can intersperse the pins and snap or barrel swivels between the charms to create the links of your bracelet. Fill the pins and swivels with beads too. Measure the bracelet on your wrist as you create and use one of the decorated pins as your fastener.

barrel swivel

snap swivel

Dancin' Queens

Are you tired of the Hokey Pokey? Fed up with the Chicken Dance? Bummed out by the Bunny Hop? Teach your feet these fun, cool steps and you'll be dancing all night.

West Coast Swing

You'll need a partner for this one! This dance originated in the 1940s and has an 8-beat step.

1. Join hands and face each other.
2. Starting with your right foot, rock to the right with quick, small steps: move right foot, left foot, right foot (1-2-3). (Your partner will move left while you move right.)
3. Starting with your left foot, rock to the left with quick, small steps: move left foot, right foot, left foot (4-5-6). (Your partner will move right this time.)
4. Rock back on your right foot for 1 beat (beat 7).
5. Rock forward on your left foot for 1 beat (beat 8).
6. Repeat. You can add 6-beat turns and twirls and then rock back and forth on the last 2 beats.

Electric Slide

Groove with the smooth steps of the coolest line dance around.

1. Grapevine to the right for 4 beats. (Step right foot to the right, step left foot behind right foot, step right foot to right, step left foot to meet your right.)

2. Grapevine to the left for 4 beats. (Step left foot to the left, step right foot in back of left foot, step left foot to the left, step right foot to meet your left.)

3. Starting with your right foot, walk backward for 4 steps.

4. With left foot forward, lean forward for 1 beat, lean back for 1 beat, lean forward again and make a quarter turn to your left.

5. Repeat.

THE GRAPEVINE

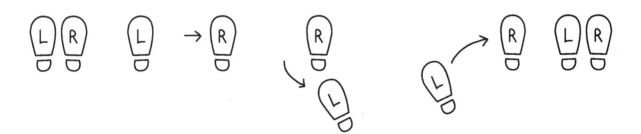

Hand Jive

The song "Willie and the Hand Jive" is by George Thorogood & The Destroyers and can be found on their 1985 album entitled *Maverick*.

1. Slap both hands on thighs 2 times.
2. Clap hands together 2 times.
3. Cross right hand over left hand 2 times.
4. Cross left hand over right hand 2 times.
5. Make fists. Hit right fist on top of left fist 2 times.
6. Hit left fist on top of right fist 2 times.
7. Point right thumb over right shoulder for 2 beats.
8. Point left thumb over left shoulder for 2 beats.
9. Repeat.

The Best Friend Hustle

Stand facing your friend and get ready to boogie. This is a version of the classic 1970s disco dance.

1. Each of you should do a 4-step grapevine to your right (so you'll be stepping away from each other). See illustration for grapevine steps on previous page. Step right foot to the right; step left foot behind right foot; step right foot to the right; bring left together with right. Clap on the last step.
2. Then grapevine to the left and toward each other. Step left foot to the left; step right foot in back of left foot; step left foot to the left; bring right foot together with left. Clap on the last step.
3. Start this pattern again, but this time start with a grapevine to the left and clap, then a grapevine to the right and clap.
4. When you meet in the middle again, bump your right hips twice, bump left hips twice.
5. Repeat and add as many crazy hand movements as you can dream up.

Mush Making!

What is "mush," you ask? Mush is that ooey, gooey, sticky, soft stuff that you and your friend can poke and pull, shape and squash. In general, it's squishable material that you can make yourselves. From the mixing to the mashing, you're going to have fun making mush. Here are several different types for you to try.

Oingo Boingo Puddy Mush

This is all-purpose mush!

You will need
- 1 cup white glue
- 1½ cups liquid starch (from the grocery store)
- A few drops of food coloring
- Medium bowl
- Plastic wrap
- Jar with a lid

Mix all of the ingredients together in a bowl with your hands. Cover the bowl with plastic wrap and let it sit for several hours. If there is any liquid starch left in the bowl, pour it out. When you're done working with the Puddy Mush, store it in a jar with a lid.

Sweet Smellin' Mush

For squeaky, clean sculptures, make some Sweet Smellin' Mush. You may want to double the recipe, depending on the size of your creations.

You will need
- 2 cups soap flakes
- ¼ cup cold water
- Medium bowl
- Glitter (optional)

Mix the flakes and the water in the bowl by squeezing them together with your hands. You can add glitter now if you'd like. When it begins to stick together, form the mixture into whatever shape you like. This stuff dries quickly, so you'll need to work rather quickly. Additional drops of water will help if the mixture gets dry. Place your finished form in the refrigerator to harden.

Munchable Mush

This is nutty dough that you can mold and munch on.

You will need
- Mixing bowl
- ½ cup smooth peanut butter
- ½ cup powdered sugar
- ½ cup white corn syrup
- 1½ cups powdered milk

Wash your hands before mixing this mush. Mix the peanut butter, powdered sugar, and white corn syrup together in the bowl. Toss in the powdered milk, and pull and squish the mixture until it is smooth. You may add a little more powdered milk if it is too sticky. Play around with the mush for as long as you like. Gobble some down when the mood strikes you! Throw away any remaining dough when you are finished.

How Well Do You Know Your Friends?

You may think you know every detail of your friends' lives—their favorite music, clothes, movie stars, and food. But this game will test the friendship IQ of even the best of pals. You create the game so you determine the level of difficulty. No matter what the level, this is a very fun way to learn even more about the people you spend so much time with!

You will need
- 4 or more friends
- 2 pieces of poster board or large paper
- Paper
- Markers or pens
- Tape

First, decide upon categories (you'll need as many categories as you have players). The categories can cover any topic of life that you'd like. We picked these categories for our game: Childhood Memories, Family, Hollywood, and Sports.

Once you have made your decisions, write the title of each category at the top of the

poster board. Now each player will write a question about herself for every category (in this case, four questions). Write each question on a folded piece of paper, place your name on the front, and tape it to the appropriate place on the chart.

Examples of questions
Childhood Memories: At what age did Liz learn to walk? What was Lisa's favorite toy?

Family: How old is Liz's little brother Michael? Where was Lisa born?

Hollywood: What is Liz's all-time favorite movie? Which movie star would Lisa most like to meet?

Sports: Who is Liz's favorite pro football player? Name Lisa's favorite Olympic sport.

To play, simply pick one player to go first. She will ask for one name other than herself and one category (for example, Liz and Hollywood). Then Liz will read that question out loud and the other players will guess the correct answer. Play until all the questions are gone. We bet that by the time you've finished, you'll know each other even better.

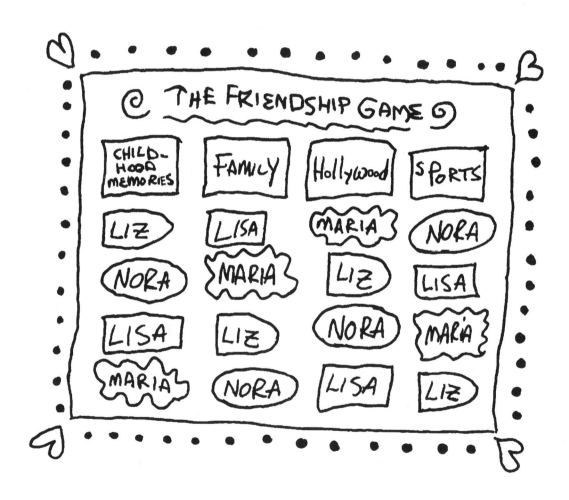

Sweetheart Sock Hop

In the 1950s, Americans were having a ball "rockin' around the clock" to music by Bill Haley and the Comets, Fats Domino, Jerry Lee Lewis, Chubby Checker, and the King himself, Elvis Presley. Huge dance parties were held in gyms across the country and became known as "Sock Hops" when the dancers started kicking off their shoes! Kids were really hopping in their letter sweaters, poodle skirts, leather jackets, and blue jeans.

Invite some friends over around Valentine's Day for a Sweetheart Sock Hop. Tell them to don their bobby socks and saddle shoes, pop their hair into a ponytail or slick it back, and be ready to rumble!

Golden Oldies Invitations

You will need
- Drinking glass
- Pencil
- Colored construction paper
- Scissors
- Black marker
- Glue
- 8- or 9-inch black plastic disposable plates (like paper plates, but thicker; you can purchase them at a party shop)
- Metallic paint pens
- Valentine stickers

Using a glass and a pencil, trace perfect circles on the construction paper and cut them out. With a black marker, color a circle about the size of a half-dollar in the very center of each construction paper circle. Glue one construction paper circle onto the center of each black plastic plate. With the black marker again, write the title of a popular song from the fifties like "Rockin' Robin" or "Great Balls of Fire" around the circle. Using your metallic pen, write the party details like when, where, and who on the black plate. Don't forget to tell your guests to wear a costume if you want them to! It's also a good idea to include your phone number in case anyone has any questions. Add the Valentine's Day stickers and then hand deliver to your party pals!

The Details
You will need to hold your Sock Hop in an area where people can dance. Basements, clean garages, or recreational rooms are super places for your party, or ask permission to move some family room furniture out of the way.

The Decorations
You can decorate for the Sock Hop by stringing crepe paper streamers about. Add some Valentine's Day balloons or cardboard cutouts of hearts and cupids to set the mood. We like hanging some golden oldies records from the streamers for a really rockin' effect!

The Music
You will need a stereo or a boom box to play music. Check out your family's music collection (your parents might even have some old records), your library, or music store for some fifties music. Many record stores have CDs and tapes that have songs from a specific decade. Try to get your hands on one that has Elvis, Jerry Lee, Chubby, and Fats for a whole lot of dancing fun!

The Menu
You can go all out and serve munchies just like the drive-ins used to make!
Boppin' Burgers
French Fries
Sody Pop
Ice Cream Cherry Bombs (recipe below)

Ice Cream Cherry Bombs

You will need

- Cupcake liners
- Cupcake or muffin pan
- Ice cream scoop
- Vanilla ice cream
- Maraschino cherries with long stems
- Bowl of chocolate syrup that hardens

With clean hands, place cupcake liners in the cupcake or muffin pan. Scoop out a small blob of ice cream, about the size of a golf ball. Working quickly, bury a cherry in the center of the ice cream ball. The stem should stick out of the top. Dip the ball into the bowl of chocolate syrup and cover all of the sides. Immediately place the Cherry Bomb onto one of the cupcake liners and place the pan in the freezer. Keep the finished Cherry Bombs cold while you work on more. Serve the Cherry Bombs straight from the freezer.

Saddle Shoe Shuffle Game

This game is a lot of fun to play. All you need to do is mark two lines on the floor with masking tape at opposite ends of the room. Divide your guests into two teams and have each team stand behind opposite lines. Have your guests take off their shoes and leave the laces untied. Put all of the shoes in a big pile in the center of the room. (To be fair, the pile should be exactly halfway between the team lines.) Give the shoes a good mix. When you say "Let's go, Daddy O!" everyone should run to the pile, find their shoes, put them on, tie the laces, and then run to the area behind their line and sit down. The first team to have every member sitting down behind their line (with their shoes on and tied) wins.

Bio-Poem

Have fun penning a poem about one of your favorite subjects—a good friend. Friends can write them for each other, and then share the piece when finished. If you are exchanging a journal with someone, perhaps a long distance friend, this would make an excellent entry.

A Bio-poem goes like this
Line 1: Your friend's full, formal name
Line 2: Four words that describe your friend
Line 3: "Lover of…" one thing or idea
Line 4: "Believes in…" OR "Believed…"
Line 5: "Who gave…" OR "Who said…"
(a quote)
Line 6: Your friend's nickname

For example
Amelia Earhart
Courageous, aviator, determined, pioneer
Lover of the wild, blue yonder
Believed that women should take flight
Who gave her life for exploration
Lady Lindy

Now it's your turn to write one.
Line 1:
Line 2:
Line 3:
Line 4:
Line 5:
Line 6:

YOU GO, GIRLS!

Biographies are nonfiction books that tell the story of someone's life. Pick up a biography about one of these important women at your school or public library. Be dazzled by their courage, ingenuity, and perseverance. Girls can do anything they set their minds to! Girl Power!

Amelia Earhart –
famous female aviator

Rosa Parks –
civil rights pioneer

Anne Frank –
teenager during the Holocaust and courageous author

Sojourner Truth –
former slave and suffragist, worked for women's rights

Clara Barton –
founder of the Red Cross

Harriet Tubman –
helped slaves escape to freedom

Mother Jones –
fought for coal miners' rights

Rachel Carson –
environmentalist and naturalist

Jane Addams –
worked for social reform and women's rights

Mother Theresa –
friend of the poor

Funky Friendship Greeting Cards

Birthdays, holidays, or any-old-day-cards are a great way to tell a friend how much you care. These cards are especially funny because they feature your friend in crazy situations. You can put your friend's face on the bodies of various characters to create a story. Be as wild as you'd like! These cards are meant to test your funny bone.

You will need
- Scissors
- Photographs of friends that can be cut up
- Old magazines
- Glue
- Construction paper
- Hole punch
- Ribbon

1. Think about the story you'd like to tell. For example, I could tell a story about Liz traveling all over the world to celebrate her birthday. Outline the story in your head or on a piece of paper and determine how many pictures and pages you will need.

2. Pull out your photographs and cut closely around your friend's face so that only the neck, face, and hair are showing. Now you can flip through magazines to find bodies that will create a funny match with your friend's face. Don't worry if the faces are not in proportion with the magazine bodies—that's half the fun! For example, I'll show Liz riding a unicycle through Paris and making pizzas in Chicago.

3. Glue these faces onto the bodies you've cut out of magazines and set aside. To make the card itself, fold each piece of your construction paper in half. Layer the folded pieces on top of one another to make a book.

4. When you have enough face and body combinations to tell your story, begin gluing them into your card. Leave room to write funny captions beneath each picture.

5. Write a poem or story to go with the pictures (even one-word captions will work). Color and decorate the card to your heart's desire. Punch two holes on the left-hand edge of the card, string a ribbon through, and tie a bow on the outside edge.

Example

There once was a girl named Liz,
For whom riding a bike was a whiz,
She never fell down,
Riding all over town,
Toting pizza and sporting a frizz.

real picture here →

magazine cutout here →

Sweet Treat Pizza

Did you know that pizza is America's favorite food? You may have eaten many tasty pizzas in your lifetime, but this one takes the cake—so to speak! Bake this with a friend and let her choose the special candy bar toppings.

You will need

- Small and large mixing bowl
- Measuring cup
- ½ cup flour
- ½ teaspoon baking soda
- ¼ teaspoon salt
- 1¼ sticks of butter, softened
- ½ cup sugar
- ½ cup packed brown sugar
- Mixing spoon or electric mixer
- 1 egg
- ½ teaspoon vanilla extract
- 1 package (12 oz.) semi-sweet chocolate chips
- Cookie sheet
- ½ cup peanut butter
- Spoon
- 1 cup of your favorite candy bars, broken into tiny pieces

Preheat the oven to 375 degrees. Be sure to ask an adult's permission before using the oven. In the small bowl, mix the flour, baking soda, and salt and set aside. In the large bowl, beat the butter, sugar, and brown sugar until creamy. Beat in the egg and vanilla extract. Slowly beat in the flour mixture from the small bowl. Stir in one cup of chocolate chips. Spread the batter on a lightly greased cookie sheet. Bake 20 minutes until the crust is lightly browned.

Remove the cookie crust from the oven and sprinkle the rest of the chocolate chips over the crust. Drop the peanut butter by spoonfuls on the melting chips. Let this stand for 5 minutes. Use the back of your spoon to gently spread the chocolate and peanut butter mixture. Decorate with crumbled candy bars and serve to hungry friends.

Music Mix Masters

Maybe your friend is a little bit country, and you're a little bit rock 'n' roll. Or maybe you prefer hip hop and she's into more alternative music. To be Music Mix Masters, all you need is music and it does not matter what kind. The more creativity you can bring to this project, the better. So crank up the tunes and let your imagination go!

You will need
- Stereo and a boom box or cassette player or 2 boom boxes (You must be able to play and record music at the same time.)
- Blank cassette tape
- Variety of CDs, cassettes, or record albums (Those hard black discs your parents have stored in the closet!)
- Paper
- Pencils

Spend some time familiarizing yourself with your music. Look over the titles. Listen for catchy refrains or phrases within the songs that really stand out. Jot these down on a piece of paper. Then write a short script, inserting interesting or funny parts of songs here and there. An interview is a fun script for two friends. The interviewer asks the questions and the subject of the interview's answers can be both spoken word and bits of song. The answers can be fairly serious or pretty crazy!

Here is a sample script:
Interviewer: I'm on the plains of South Dakota on this beautiful second day of February awaiting the arrival of Mr. Ground Hog. Wait! I believe I see him. Mr. Hog!

Ground Hog: (From the Doors' song) *"Hello, I love you—Won't you tell me your name?"*

Interviewer: My word! This is one friendly rodent. I'm R. W. Scoop and Mr. Hog, we're all very anxious to find out if you've seen your shadow today!

Ground Hog: Well, actually I haven't gotten around to it yet. It's been pretty cloudy out here in Prairie Dog Land, but hang on a minute . . . (From the Beatles' song) *"Here comes the sun! Here comes the sun and I say, it's alright."*

Interviewer: Well, isn't this fantastic? We are actually witnessing Mr. Ground Hog searching for his shadow. But, whoa! What's that over there? It appears to be a large group of bikers headed our way! Mr. Hog, head for your hole! (Thump!) Oh, the humanity! Mr. Hog has been knocked on the head by a reckless biker. Let me see if I can get closer. Mr. Hog, are you okay?

Ground Hog: Yeah, I'm okay. (From the Chumbawumba song) *"I get knocked down, but I get up again! You're never gonna keep me down!"*

Interviewer: Well, this reporter finds it refreshing to see a creature take their Ground Hog Day responsibilities so seriously. It has been a pleasure, Mr. Hog.

And so on, and so on!

Practice reading your written script a couple of times. When you're ready to record, begin reading the script aloud into the microphone of your stereo, boom box, or cassette player. When you come to a spot where you need to insert music, press pause (on the recording device) and cue up the part of the song that you want to tape (on the other boom box or stereo.) Record that piece of the song and then press the pause button again when you're done.

Remember, the song bits will be brief— probably just a well-known line from a song or a short refrain. Continue reading, recording, and inserting parts of songs until you reach the end of the script. Rewind the tape and listen to your masterful music mixing!

Mardi Gras

Mardi Gras is an exciting, colorful celebration held in many countries that have Catholic communities, although people of many different religions like to take part in the fun! The day of Mardi Gras depends on the date of Easter, so it's different each year. You and your best friend can have a great time on Mardi Gras, which is held on the Tuesday before Lent begins. Mardi Gras is a French word that means "Fat Tuesday." Many years ago, a fat ox was paraded through the streets of Paris on the day before Lent. People would feast on good food and have merry parties on this day before fasting began. Soon after, they started calling the day, "Fat Tuesday."

French colonists introduced Mardi Gras to America in the early 1700s. Today, the city of New Orleans holds a grand Mardi Gras party with huge parades, beautiful floats, loud marching bands, and fancy costume balls. People wear outrageous masks and costumes and march in the parades. Candy and colorful bead necklaces are tossed to the people in the crowds. Join the celebration by making these feather masks, donning some beads, feasting on some delicious food, and remember, as the Cajuns say, to "Laissez les bon temps rouler!" (In English, "Let the good times roll!")

MARDI GRAS MAGIC

For a taste of Mardi Gras in full-blown color, check out *Mardi Gras!* by Suzanne M. Coil. The photographs by Mitchel Osborne are spectacular!

Feather Masks

You will need

- Mask outline (see below)
- Pencil
- Waxed paper
- Scissors
- Cardboard
- Glue
- Pretty feathers (from a craft or fabric store)
- Sequins
- Paper punch
- String

1. Place the waxed paper over the mask outline on this page and trace it. Cut it out.

2. Use this waxed paper outline to trace a mask onto the cardboard. Cut this out.

3. Glue the feathers onto the cardboard mask. You may want to cut the feathers in half sometimes. Make an interesting pattern of overlapped feathers.

4. Glue sequins around the mask in pretty patterns.

5. Allow the glue to dry and then punch holes on each side of the mask.

6. Tie a short length of string to each side of the mask. Have your friend help you to make sure the strings will go around your head and tie in the back.

7. Voila! You now have fancy feather masks for Mardi Gras!

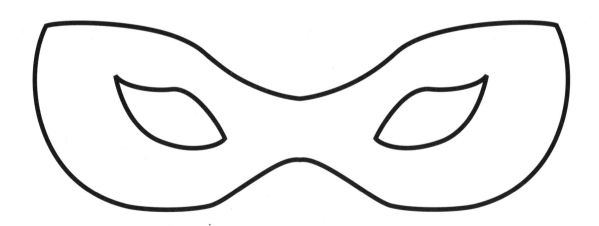

trace outline of mask

We think New Orleans has some of the best food around! French, Spanish, and African influences on Louisiana cooking have created an interesting menu. Have you ever tasted jambalaya? It is a spicy dish with sausage and rice. Some other traditional and tasty dishes include gumbo, a stew of meats, vegetables, and okra, and muffulettas, a meat and cheese sandwich with an olive and pepper dressing. When in New Orleans, you might try red beans and rice or boiled crawfish. For dessert, visitors to "The Big Easy" (another nickname for this laid-back town) can enjoy a pecan candy called a praline, or beignets, which are like rich doughnuts. Another popular treat is a Po-Boy and we've included an easy recipe for you and your friend to try!

Po-Boy Sandwiches
Serves 2

You will need
- Loaf of French bread
- Serrated knife
- Cutting board
- Mayonnaise
- 10 slices of turkey or ham from the deli
- Tomato slices
- 1 cup shredded lettuce

Slice the bread in half like a hot dog bun. Spread mayonnaise on both halves of the bread. Lay the meat slices down on one half. When ordering a Po-Boy, many people ask for it "dressed." This means they want lettuce, tomatoes, and mayonnaise. Dress your Po-Boy by adding some tomato slices and shredded lettuce. Put the top on and slice the sandwich in two. There's half a Po-Boy for you and half for a friend.

Handmade Thank-You Notes

We have so much to give thanks for—trees, sun, fresh air, warm chocolate-chip cookies, backrubs, soft beds, loving families, yummy meals, loyal pets, bubble baths, music, laughter, healthy bodies, kind hearts, and, most of all, best friends. It's important to appreciate the little things in life and thank those who help you along the way. Why not pen a note to the kind people who assisted you with some of the activities in this book? The mom who let you play slumber party games, the dad who helped you hang balloons for your Sweetheart Sock Hop, and the neighbor who lent you her yard for a carnival would love a handmade thank-you from the heart.

You will need
- Construction paper
- Scissors
- Rubber stamps and ink
- Markers or crayons

Cut your construction paper into any shape or size you choose. Consider the personality of the person you are thanking and design your card around something they like—fish for a fisherman or flowers for a gardener. Simply fold your card in half and fill the inside with your thoughts and feelings, a poem you've written, or a great quote you've found. Decorate with rubber stamps or markers.

Here's a little thank-you we wrote for you:

Dear Friends,

We want to thank you for exploring the activities in our book! It makes us happy knowing that you are out there having fun with your girlfriends. Be good to one another and enjoy yourselves.

Love,
Lisa and Liz

Bibliography

Bondi, Victor. *American Decades 1940–1949*. Gale Research Inc., 1995.

Drucker, Malka. *Hanukkah: Eight Nights, Eight Lights*. Holiday House, 1980.

Encarta '96 Encyclopedia. Microsoft Corporation, 1996.

Gascoigne, Marc. *You Can Surf the Net!* Penguin Group, 1995.

Hirsch, E. D., J. F. Kett, and J. Trefil. *The Dictionary of Cultural Literacy*. Houghton Mifflin Company, 1993.

Mahnken, Jan. *The Backyard Bird-Lover's Guide*. Storey Communications, 1996.

Medearis, Angela Shelf. *The Seven Days of Kwanzaa*. Scholastic Inc., 1994.

Powell, Jillian. *Traditions Around the World*. Thomson Learning, 1995.

Stepanchuk, Carol. *Red Eggs and Dragon Boats*. Pacific View Press, 1995.

Wallner, Alexandra. *Ghoulish Giggles and Monster Riddles*. Albert Whitman & Company, 1982.

Winchester, Faith. *African-American Holidays*. Capstone Press, 1996.

Wright, David, and Elly Petra. *America in the 20th Century 1950-1959*. Marshall Cavendish Press, 1995.